Freedom Fighters

Affective Teaching of the Language Arts

Second Edition

Nancy Lee Cecil

California State University, Sacramento

Sheffield Publishing Company

Salem, Wisconsin

For information about this book, write or call:
Sheffield Publishing Company
P.O. Box 359
Salem, Wisconsin 53168
(414) 843-2281

ISBN 1-879215-22-5

Printed in the United States of America

7 6 5 4 3 2 1

DEDICATION

With love...and hearts and princesses and rainbows...to Chrissy, who is teaching me what the learning process is **REALLY** all about.

Contents

FREEDOM FIGHTERS:

Affective Teaching of the
Language Arts, 2/E

Anecdotal Outline

Preface.

similar rhythm and rhyming patterns, and offers an opportunity for children to collaborate on classroom books. Specific suggestions are offered for applying this method to nine children's books, and a bibliography of appropriate "predictable" books is included in Appendix I.

4 **Episodic Novels: Becoming REAL Authors.** Described here is the more ambitious and self-motivating experience of writing a class-collaborative novel by following a brief outline of chapters, brainstorming each chapter as a class, and then breaking up into "think" groups to finish individual chapters. A sample highly-motivational, field-tested outline is provided.

5 **Other Motivators: When They Don't Know What to Write.** A panoply of story starters, story plots, and other "getting started" ideas are presented in this chapter to spur initial creative attempts. Also included is a test of creativity, and some general suggestions designed to foster creativity in all areas of the curriculum.

6 **Build-Me-Ups: Enhancing Self-Concept Through the Language Arts.** Explored here are a host of language activities that are specifically focused upon improving the self-images of children. Acceptance of cultural and socioeconomic differences, and valuing what is "unique" in people are highlighted in such proposed activities as "Good or Bad?" and the "You Are Special Because ..." Circle.

7 **The Newspaper: Conduit to Our Reading Culture.** This chapter demonstrates many ways to make children feel comfortable with the newspaper through activities designed to develop their critical reading, thinking, and writing abilities. A newspaper scavenger hunt, writing headlines, and doing interviews with lottery winners are among the activities included.

for whom English is a second language, to express ideas. This final chapter offers teachers suggestions as to how drama, singing, music, art, photography and dance can become potent paths to literacy.

Preface

The second edition of *Freedom Fighters*, like the previous edition, is designed to help teachers create an affective, whole-language program that will free ALL children to communicate unself-consciously and to then give them plenty of motivational reasons to continue to do so. Such a program has as its foundation the fervent belief that reading, writing, listening, and speaking are naturally interacting processes that can be joyously occurring all day long, spilling into every other nook and cranny of the elementary curriculum.

Revisions in this Edition

The second edition includes a discrete chapter on integrating literacy and the arts. The purpose of such an inclusion is to provide additional perspective on the variety of ways children can learn and share what they know. Based upon the groundbreaking "Theory of Multiple Intelligence" espoused by cognitive psychologist Howard Gardner, this chapter offers exciting strategies to blend the two, making learning meaningful, satisfying and accessible to all learners in today's heterogeneous classrooms. The integration of literacy and the arts offers caring teachers yet another set of avenues through which they can reach ALL their learners, regardless of how each child's intelligence manifests itself.

Additionally, this new edition provides much new information on the specific needs of second-language learners. Although the text has been designed with the entire spectrum of learners in mind, I have found that teachers are continually searching for new ideas to help them meet the social, emotional, and linguistic needs of the diverse learners that now enter their classrooms in increasingly large numbers. Many helpful tools for reaching linguistically diverse learners are contained in this edition.

Finally, since writing the first edition of *Freedom Fighters*, I have discovered many new and innovative ideas designed to motivate reluctant learners, more information about affective whole-language instruction, and even a few new vocabulary-enhancing activities. This new information has been incorporated into this updated text. While all of the new and previously proffered ideas have been field-tested and proven successful in multilingual classrooms, the reader should keep in mind that what works well with one class may not work as well with another. Similarly, ideas that are suitable for one grade level may need specific adaptations to make them suitable for another. I trust the competent teacher, who knows the children best, to make these judgments.

Acknowledgements

I would like to thank everyone who has made both the first and second editions of this book possible. My husband, Gary, read drafts and offered constructive feedback and encouragement. My daughter, Chrissy, tried out many ideas and gave her enthusiastic approval. Steve Nelson, my editor, took a chance on this book because of his commitment to literacy for his own children and everyone else's. My preservice teachers affirmed the ideas, tried them in their placements, and shared the results with me. Finally, a host of incredible affective teachers in Sacramento provided ample opportunities for consultation, inservice, and workshops to refine the ideas. This book would never have been written without the input of these individuals.

I believe that helping all children to become literate is the most exciting, rewarding, and IMPORTANT mission upon which a person could ever embark. Most readers of this text are beginning such an adventure or are currently undertaking it. My personal wish is that this text can make your path a bit smoother as you bring to life the ideas of this text in your own special ways. For now, more than ever before, the caring teacher must be the veritable "freedom fighter," arming learners with the ability to communicate freely and confidently in a challenging world.

Introduction

What is the significance of language for a small child? To answer that question, one must only listen to young Anthony, who is learning all about the power that language is beginning to hold for him. Anthony is learning how to pose questions and he does so interminably. He is learning how to get his needs met and he practices endlessly. He now knows how to give commands to his dog—and even his baby brother—and he revels in the responses he can now cause. Anthony is also becoming aware of the many rituals of our language and he finds that chirping "Have a nice day!" coupled with his sunny, gap-toothed grin, may soften even the grumpiest of adults.

Language, simply put, is the systematic ability to communicate and understand the communication of others. This ability to communicate is pure, unadulterated power. But without this power a child can easily be the victim of other children, of teachers, of the school, and of virtually the whole society outside the child's home environment. A child who lacks this communication facility remains largely on the fringe of all social interaction; on the fringe of all life. Without the ability to communicate—and the tremendous FREEDOM it affords—the child is locked into a netherworld between the stimulating world of voices and print and the frustrating chains of his own powerlessness.

What is needed to best impart this important power to children is an "affective" approach to the teaching of the language arts—that is, an approach that reaches right to the **heart** of the learner. Such an approach regards communication as the most basic human need to interact with others on a very real emotional, as well as intellectual, level. Therefore, the affective

1

teacher of language arts—the arts of reading, writing, speaking and listening—will be viewed in this book as the ultimate Freedom Fighter, sensitively preparing her students to one day participate in the twenty-first century by freeing them to communicate effectively. Such a teacher must be well aware of the unique nature of this charge, for the ability to communicate is the most personal, human, and profoundly vulnerable of the tools a child will need to succeed. It also takes much long practice, yet touches every aspect of the child's environment. By freeing the child, the affective teacher allows that child to grow by following his or her own thoughts in oral or written form. The affective teacher helps the child to "... unlock the doors of language...to discover the best that human beings have thought, written and spoken" (California State Board of Education, 1987).

Unfortunately, much of what goes on in our elementary classrooms has quite the opposite effect from offering our children the freedom to communicate. For example, a perplexed teacher consulted me recently about her observation that her third-grade students seemed to dislike writing; they appeared to be producing less and less writing than they had been at the very beginning of the school year. She showed me an example of young Barbara's latest composition and it soon became quite clear what the problem was—the child's composition was awash with red marks and curt marginal admonitions. Every misspelled word, uncapitalized letter, or bit of improper grammar or punctuation had been conscientiously circled and sarcastically chastised. But the saddest thing of all was that not a mention—not **one word**—had been made of the original thoughts that Barbara had been trying to communicate! Is it any wonder that this child's creative juices were "drying up"?

Similarly, I observed a "Show and Tell" session not long ago in which a very timid first-grader was trying to tell the class about her very scary adventure on Halloween. The little girl could barely finish a sentence before the teacher would pounce upon the child's grammar or word pronunciation, and then would ask the little girl to now ..."repeat the sentence the proper way." The teacher later confided to me that her pupils seemed to have nothing to say in Show and Tell, yet they ... "are little chatterboxes when they are supposed to be doing their workbook pages!"

The above anecdotes are unfortunate and all-too-familiar examples of well-meaning teachers who are unknowingly restricting the language powers of children when they should be freeing them by allowing them to become more fluent communicators through practicing with their own ideas. An affective teacher is, of course, also concerned with arming her students with the necessary skills involved in the language arts. Skills in grammar, capitalization, spelling, reading and listening for specific purposes, and punctuation, for example, are all mechanics, or "tools of the trade," and are vital for the pupil who is to be successful in future academic endeavors. But an affective teacher of the language arts could never interrupt a child's natural exhilaration when the creative ideas are flowing and the child's mind is racing ahead of her mouth or her pen. Instead, in an affective language arts program, skill instruction takes a subservient position to the decidedly more exciting enterprise of capturing, somehow, what one is trying to communicate. This is the crucial focus—this freeing of the child's thoughts—and the mechanics can surely be scrutinized and then cleaned up in a later, less emotional moment, when the child has finished creating and now wants to share her "magnum opus" with the rest of the world. Often, using this approach of "create now, edit later," the most amazing thing happens: the child feels free to express herself and begins to write unself-consciously. The more unself-conscious she becomes, the more she begins to pay more careful attention to the writing of others and the conventions (mechanics!) of our language. While I would not go so far as to say that the mechanics then take care of themselves, I can heartily avow that significant growth will just naturally take place in the mechanics of a youngster who writes often and joyfully.

To allow burgeoning, unself-conscious communicators to flourish to maximum fluency, the language arts program must permeate every single hour of the child's day. Language arts must not be trivialized into discrete packages of reading, writing, spelling, handwriting, literature, language, etc., but must blend and flow into every nook and cranny of the curriculum. In a truly affective, whole language program, oral language is happening all day long and might take the form of discussions, debates, drama, interviews or twenty questions. Social studies might be the vehicle through which a "rap" on current events is performed, or a writing lesson is undertaken about how a passing butterfly could have changed the events of the Boston Tea Party. In such a program, too, literature is constantly being interwoven to motivate and to personalize learning in all subjects, for to exclude it from the language arts program is to ... "create a program that deprives children of their right to improve their language in the most honest and enjoyable way" (Coody and Nelson, 1986). In an Affective Language Arts Program, simply put, "language arts" is happening all the time so that no one segment of the school day need arbitrarily be labeled "language arts times." As an added bonus to such a joyful program, it should be noted that current research suggests that the more the language arts are carefully coordinated or correlated with each other and with other academic instruction, the greater the total achievement of the students will be!

*   *   *   *   *

The following chapters will give specific suggestions for creating an affective whole language, cross-curricular program which will free children to communicate and then give them plenty of motivational reasons to continue to do so. Of course, the key to this program, as in any sound educational program, is a knowledgeable and caring teacher who can capably model a love for language. He must be able to share the bittersweet experience of finishing a stirring book that he wished would never end; he should be able to express to his students the glee that is his when he finds just the right word to express what he wants to say; and he must desperately want to free his students by helping them to develop that same fine power to communicate effectively.

This book is for him. And for all the other Freedom Fighters in our schools today.

References

Anderson, Richard, et al. *Becoming a Nation of Readers.* 1985.

Coody, Betty and David Nelson. *Teaching Elementary Language Arts.* Prospect Heights, IL: Waveland Press, 1986.

California State Board of Education. *English-Language Arts Framework.* Sacramento, CA: California State Department of Education, 1986.

Chapter One

Writing: Process and Product

Although writing is closely linked to its "cousin" language arts—speaking, reading, and listening—a child who is able to tell a wonderfully bone-chilling story with aptly descriptive words and finely-tuned phrases may often have major problems when it comes to writing down such stories. The observers of this phenomenon are perplexed. If writing and oral language are so closely linked, as we are led to believe, then why is it that the child speaks so articulately and yet cannot write fluently?

First of all, good writing has the same general qualities whether it is the scribbled composition of the second graders or the carefully-crafted essay of the adult writer. Learning to express oneself is always a meticulous, time-consuming process—perhaps the most difficult of the communication skills, and it basically subsumes all the others: writing requires the combined ability to talk and form sentences, to read, to make letters, to spell, to punctuate, and to think clearly and logically. Also, there is the tough physical labor of getting the material down. While an animated nine-year-old may speak as many as two hundred words per minute, she will be doing well to write that many in an hour!

Secondly, the practice ratio of time spent on speaking as compared with time spent on writing in a young child's life is very much in the favor of speaking time, in all but the rarest of cases. Perhaps because conversation is not usually structured for them, children talk a **lot**. In every facet of their environment, children seem to have new opportunities to practice their oral language, but unfortunately, the same myriad of opportunities do not exist for language in written form. In many cases, the only writing practice children will have in a day will be the practice of identifying parts of speech and putting one line under the subject and two under the predicate in their "language" books!

Lastly, there is the important issue of positive reinforcement. Picture in your mind the four-year-old who stumbles and stutters over his words in youthful exuberance to tell his parents about his trip to the circus, or the preschooler who makes up a story about a "wed wabbit." Now picture the reaction of the adults as they listen to these children. Invariably, there will be a positive, even indulgent response to this immature speech. Unfortunately, no such indulgence greets the immature writer when he rushes home with his first rudimentary attempts to write. Somehow, we seem to expect children to go from being nonwriters to perfectly literate authors in one quantum leap!

The bottom line is that writing is a most difficult task requiring a good deal of varied practice, and the beginning writer's first feeble attempt at the craft must be thoughtfully accepted and encouraged from the perspective of what we now know of the developmental process of a child's written language.

Invented Spellings

This knowledge has led to increased attention placed on the value of accepting a beginning writer's "invented spellings." Invented spellings are the combinations of letters that a young child uses when he is just beginning to understand that letters represent the sounds that form words. These novel spellings that a child has created by sounding out words are not "errors," although they are not actually "correct" according to our whimsical English orthography. Rather, they are really immaturities that show the developmental stage the child is at in terms of his knowledge of the way sounds and symbols come together in our language. By allowing these invented spellings in the initial stages of writing, children become free to communicate anything they can conjure up in their fertile imaginations, while it also provides the best opportunity for them to extend their knowledge of phonics, or the way that letters and sounds correspond.

In learning to communicate in written form, a child generally goes through five basic developmental stages, although it is not uncommon for children to evidence elements of two or more of these stages in their writing at any one time.

The Precommunicative Stage

The first stage of such development is the precommunicative stage and it occurs about the time that a child learns the alphabet and makes the connection that words are composed of letters, although the child has little or no concept at the time of which letter stands for which sound. A child at this stage might compose a story about an elephant and to our eyes it will be virtually unintelligible:

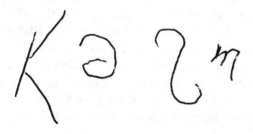

The Prephonetic Stage

The second stage of development is called the prephonetic stage and it evolves when a child begins to understand that letters have certain sounds which form words. About this time, too, children are usually beginning to become aware of the left-to-right orientation of our language. This particular writing stage might be considered analogous to the stage in a very young child's beginning speech when he will use one word to symbolize a whole concept, such as "Up!" to mean "I want you to pick me up!" Similarly, in this particular stage, one letter, which is often the most obvious sound, will be used to represent the whole word. In the previously used story about the elephant, the word elephant would merely be represented by an "1," its most salient auditory feature. The whole story might look like this:

i ω ⊇ C L

The Phonetic Stage

The third stage, the phonetic stage, is in some ways just a refinement of the prephonetic stage, except now a letter will be used for each sound that a child can hear in each syllable. Although vowels and silent letters may often be left out, the child seems to have become aware of some of the most basic word patterns and families in our language (e.g. fab, cab, hat). Now the same story about an elephant might look like this:

I wnt To the zunDswnelfnt

The Transitional Stage

The fourth developmental stage is called the transitional stage and at this phase children's writing is quite coherent, as children begin to have a repertoire of words that have been taught to them and everything need not be sounded out. At this stage, too, children have usually begun to read, so they are now more aware of the words' more visual aspects, some of which would not be detectable to the ear. Vowels begin to be placed in each syllable at this stage, and common English sequences such as the "ai" in "rain" and "pain," begin to emerge in the child's spelling. The elephant story might now become:

I went to the zoo and saw an ellefent

Correct Spelling

The final stage of writing development, that of correct spelling, evolves when the child is tuned in to the idiosyncrasies of English orthography and just "knows" by sight if a word is spelled correctly. Now the child's spelling shows an understanding of contraction, affixes, silent letters, and he or she has a great many words that can be spelled as automatically as the child's own name.

Keeping these developmental stages in mind, as well as the value of a child's use of invented spellings, may help the teacher decide what level of writing might be expected from each child and may help to keep unrealistic expectations from inhibiting the writing process.

Before a child has reached the phonetic stage of development, the writing process should be kept as simple and unconstrained as possible. At this early stage, many opportunities should be provided for children to do art work and then tell stories about their creations in rough written form. This process could be varied by the child sometimes telling his story to the teacher as she transcribes it and with individual and group language experience stories. Also, much writing by children in these stages can be performed with plastic or metal letters on flannel boards or with primary typewriters to lessen the frustration of handwriting constraints. At these initial stages of writing, invented spelling is a worthwhile end in itself and little or no actual "editing" of children's writing should be attempted.

The Writing Process

When children are beginning to write freely, beginning to spell phonetically, as well as expressing a real desire to share their writing with others, it is time to begin turning them into true authors by introducing them to the hard work—and the ultimate joy—of editing their work with the intent to publish. They are ready to begin what is known as "the writing process."

The Creating Phase

The writing process begins with a creating phase and it is absolutely crucial to the free flow of ideas that both the teacher and the pupils realize that NO ONE—not even a published author—writes a perfect, error-free copy the first time through. The phase requires the formulation of a rough draft, or "sloppy copy," and the ideas produced in this phase remain, for the moment, in the same form in which they left the author's head. In this creating phase, the teacher facilitates by reacting in a positive, interested way to the child's ideas, and nothing else. If something in the writing, a word or phrase is unclear, the teacher asks the child if she could elaborate, but does not EVER interfere with what the child has to say. As part of the writing process, children should be urged to keep on-going personal folders of their writing so that they can choose what would be worth the effort of editing, or "polishing up," for publication. The teacher should make his students aware that everything that is written is not necessarily of the same quality; thus, every piece that has been written during the year need not be selected for publication. Therefore, self-evaluation of one's writing is also an important component of this creating phase. Children should be encouraged to choose works for publication that they feel have the best ideas, the best expression of those ideas, as well as pieces that they are very proud of and wish to share by taking the time to edit them for publication.

Self-Editing

The second phase in the writing process is the self-editing phase. Now that many creative ideas have been put on paper and the child has selected among them a work that she feels is worthy of expending more effort upon, the attention can now be directed toward any spelling, punctuation, grammatical, or capitalization concerns. Children should be encouraged to read and reread their work several times at this stage, circling errors, or putting check marks in the margins where corrections need to be made. Students might then be asked to trade their work with a trusted friend who will also help to spot additional mechanical errors.

When the child has completed the self-editing phase to the best of her ability, the work is then turned in to the teacher, who thoughtfully reads the piece and may fill out an "author's evaluation form" similar to the one on page 14.

Initial Sharing

At this stage, the child may wish to gather feedback from his/her peers by reading the piece to a small group of trusted friends. In order for this audience to be most helpful to the author, the teacher can demonstrate the use of a "Response Guide" which gives children specific comments, questions, and

Author's Evaluation Form

Title "The Horse Adventure"

Author   Juanita Quiroz

The idea I like best is I like the idea that the horse talks to many animals and an old woman. They say funny things to each other.

I'd like to hear more about what happened when they walked down the road with the black cat.

Organization:

Beginning   good - grabs my attention

Middle   lots of exciting adventures

Ending   could be more interesting

Comments   You have created a wonderful set of adventures for this horse! It was a very comical story.

praise that tends to be more valuable than a well-meaning "It was good" or "I liked it." The response guide might include such questions and comments as:

Comments	Questions
I like the part where...	Could you combine these two sentences?
I'd like to know more about...	Are your paragraphs in the right order?
Your writing made me feel...	Do you need a closing?
Your dialogue was realistic when...	Could you describe _____?
You used some powerful words, like...	Could you write a lead-in sentence to "grab" the reader?
I like the way you explained...	Could you add more to this part because...?
I especially liked the beginning because...	This part doesn't make sense to me...
I really liked the setting because...	Could you tell me more about _____?
I liked the order you used because...	Could you change these "tired" words?

To give children practice in using such a guide, the teacher may want to show children anonymous pieces of writing from former classes. The teacher can then discuss with children how to critique the writing tactfully and help them decide which questions and comments would be the most helpful and appropriate.

Additionally, at this stage, children may be ready for some peer group editing. By using the above-mentioned response guide, children can give each other helpful written (oral for younger children) feedback on the content of their work. The following is a helpful form to use for such an activity:

Peer Editing Guide

Editor:_____ Author:_____

Title of Piece:_____

1. Compliments: These are some things I really liked about
   your writing:

   _____

   _____

   _____

2. Questions: These are some things I would like to
   understand better about this piece of writing:

   _____

   _____

   _____

3. Suggestions: Here are some specific suggestions I have
   to make your writing even better:

   _____

   _____

   _____

The Writing Conference

When such a form has been completed, the teacher schedules
a writing conference with the child. The teacher begins this
conference on a very positive note by reacting to some
interesting ideas in the child's work and praises something about

it. He gives the child the distinct impression that he respects the effort that has been expended thus far in the creating and editing phases, but somehow makes it clear that the joint goal of the teacher and the author is now to make this important piece of writing even better. At that point, the teacher and child discuss the piece and the points that have been brought out in the evaluation form. During the conference, the affective teacher should always be careful to:

1) be sensitive to the author's feelings;
2) tune in to ability and developmental writing stage of the author; make sure the author is able to understand the comments;
3) use only the author's words—not the teacher's;
4) be more concerned with WHAT was said, than HOW it was said;
5) make all corrections in the presence of the author;
6) ask permission to make any major revisions.

Paragraphs

When the self-editing process has been completed and the writing conference has produced a revised piece of writing, the child is ready for the next phase, which involves deciding how to group the sentences into cohesive paragraphs and how to turn bits of narrative into dialogue by the use of quotation marks. Since the essence of a paragraph is a group of sentences that support a main idea, this concept should be pointed out with stories that are read aloud to children and in stories that children read for themselves. Then, when they are producing their own writing, paragraphs are not an unfamiliar idea. Children can be asked to reread their own work to decide which sentences go together to accompany an illustration, or which group of sentences best describe an event that is taking place. When they have selected the sentences, they should be directed to draw a large circle around them, like so:

Once there was a little
dog who wandered off into
the dark forest, not aware of   (picture)
where he was going or where
he had been.

Soon the dog came upon
a kind looking man. The dog
asked, "Sir, do you know   (picture)
where I live?" The man
answered, "No, I sure don't."

Then the man reached
down and picked up the dog,
and to the animal's surprise,   (picture)
he took him straight to the
pound!

At this point, rough sketches may be drawn of characters and
events that accompany the paragraphs. To determine what the
actual dialogue might be like, children should be encouraged to
use balloons coming from the characters' mouths, "cartoon
style," and then they should ask themselves, "What exactly
would this dog have said when that happened?" to find out where
the quotation marks would be.

Additionally, it is helpful here to provide scissors, paste and
sturdy cardboard so that writers can rearrange paragraphs by
cutting and pasting as they discover a more logical sequence for
their ideas.

Making a Cover

The fifth phase of the writing process, making a cover, is
strategically placed toward the end of the process so that children
can have a mental break (remember: they have now rewritten
their original work three or four times!) and get an inspirational

glimpse of what the final product will look like. It often provides an additional incentive to keep going with all this hard work. Now students should be encouraged to make a picture for the front cover that shows a salient feature from their work—a major event or the funniest incident—so that the important reading skill of finding the main idea is reinforced. A wide variety of methods for designing covers should be made available to children: tempera paints, felt-tip pens, tissue paper, wrapping paper, and torn bits of construction paper are all media I have seen used with excellent results. To add interest, book covers can also be cut into different shapes to enhance the ideas in the book. Animal shapes, car shapes, football shapes, or banjo shapes, for example, would provide a curious stimulation for both the writer and the future readers. Finally, lamination (by the teacher, art teacher or media specialist) then gives the finished cover more substance. Of course, actual book covers should be conspicuously on display in the writing center and pointed out during read aloud time, so that children can see the variety of titles and that the author's name is on every published work.

When an original cover has been designed with the author's name prominently in evidence on it, in most cases, wild horses could not keep a child from now completing the book! They are now ready to produce the "final copy," which means that previous revisions must be incorporated with the child's very best handwriting, which the child now has the highest motivation to use. Initially, lined paper may be used for the final copy of beginning authors, but eventually tracers should be provided so that children can produce books that look as close to the "real thing" as possible. Primary children might be instructed to place one paragraph on a page and leave plenty of room for the pictures, while older children may want to have more text on a page and fewer illustrations. When all the handsomely-polished print has been perfectly wedded to the page, children can attend to the final touches of elaborate illustrations and the very important title page. During this final phase, careful attention should be drawn to the variety of illustrations used in existing children's literature, and the importance of the illustrator should be underscored during read aloud time and as a child selects a book for recreational reading.

Publication

The final phase of the writing process is the publishing phase and it is the blissful time when young authors receive copious recognition for all the very important hard work they have just completed. In an Affective Language Arts Program, this phase is THE KEY to the success of the whole endeavor. The child has been laboring industriously with her whole mind, and she now reaps the emotional pay-off as she learns what it feels like to actually publish something that she created. Finished work should be ceremoniously put on display in the classroom for others to read, after profuse congratulations have been expressed by the teacher. A separate sheet of paper should be carefully clipped to the back of the book so that classmates can add their comments and extend "kudos" to the author. Parents can take part in the celebration if a brief note is sent home with the book so that the child can proudly read his "magnum opus" to the other members of the family. Finally, any other audiences that can be rounded up should be utilized. Other avenues for sharing the work might include reading it to other classes (kindergartners are wonderful, **adoring** listeners!), reading it over the P.A. system, to the principal or librarian, presenting it at local P.T.A. meetings, nursing homes, or sharing it with a host of other interested community groups that would be thrilled to recognize the child's achievement. Additionally, an "author's chair" should be a standard feature in an affective program where much writing is going on. It is in this very special seat that deserving writers can personally share their efforts with other class members, if they so desire.

All this recognition and applause over the child's work are the positive reinforcement that make all the hard work suddenly seem quite worthwhile. Soon other, more reluctant writers in the class observe the author's success and they, too, begin to write.

A creative renaissance is begun in the classroom and it can only lead to one more thing: **more books!**

Implications for Diverse Learners

As compared with a "transmission approach" to writing, where instruction is most concerned with handwriting, spelling, and grammar, in the writing process classroom, the children's own experiences are THE most critical issues (Farrell, 1991). Research suggests that second-language learners can benefit from such an approach where their ideas are valued over their sometimes limited ability to express them, and many opportunities for revision are offered (Au, 1993). Moreover, the writing process approach offers children a chance to choose their own topics that can emerge from their own cultural, ethnic, and linguistic backgrounds. In an affective classroom atmosphere, where children feel free to take risks and follow their own idiosyncratic paths, diverse learners have the best opportunity to thrive. Finally, second-language learners are most sensitive to the belief system that their teacher holds about writing and what's important. If the teacher clearly subscribes to the belief that rich ideas emanate from a wide variety of perspectives, children will learn to value their own culturally-based ideas. If the teacher accepts their ideas with warmth and affirmation, children who are not yet fluent with English will be eager to attempt to express complex thoughts in writing-even if they lack full command of English grammar and spelling.

Summary

Writing as a process can be tedious and very difficult for everyone, let alone the beginning writer. So to launch a writing program with the best chance of success, the affective teacher must be aware of the developmental writing stages that all children go through, so that her expectations can be appropriate to the writing ability of each of her pupils. Invented spellings should be encouraged in the early stages, until children have become confident to the degree that they are eager to write because they feel they have important things to say; they must feel free to explore print as an avenue for expressing ideas without worrying about the correctness of form. When children have reached the stage where they are able to "sound out" most words and have memorized many others, they are ready to begin the very same writing process that published authors go through.

Eventually, every child should have the freedom and the power to produce a good piece of writing that he is proud of and eager to share with the world. Such an end product takes phenomenal effort, so children must be gently guided through the writing process and encouraged to keep going when they become discouraged or frustrated with the many revisions that a good piece of writing necessarily entails. But with enough assistance along the way from an affective teacher who genuinely believes in each child and his unique ideas, a writing revolution will soon occur in such a classroom. It can be so exciting that the momentum will be self-perpetuating. As the first beautiful books are published and are met with the "oohs" and "aaahs" of classmates and admiring adults, everyone else in the class will want to write and publish and have these grand feelings of success for themselves.

References

Applegate, M. *Freeing Children to Write*. NY: Harper and Row, 1963.

Au, K. H. *Literacy Instruction in Multicultural Settings*. Fort Worth, TX: Harcourt Brace Jovanovich, 1993.

Barclay, K. "From Scribbling to 'Read Writing': What Parents and Teachers of Young Children Should Know About Literacy Development." N.L. Cecil, ed. *Literacy in the '90s*. Dubuque, IA: Kendall/Hunt, 1990.

Cecil, N.L. *Teaching to the Heart: An Affective Approach to Literacy Instruction*. 2nd ed. Salem, WI: Sheffield Publishing Co., 1993.

Cowen, J.E. *Teaching Reading Through the Arts*. Newark, DE: The International Reading Association, 1983.

Farrell, E.J. "Instructional Models for English Language Arts, K-12." J. Flood, J.M. Jensen, D. Lapp, and J.R. Squire, eds., *Handbook of Research in Teaching the English Language Arts*. NY: Macmillan, 1991, pp. 63-84.

Graves, D. *Breaking Ground: Teachers Relate Reading and Writing in the Elementary School*. Exeter, NY: Heinemann Educational Books, 1985.

Olson, C.B., ed. *Practical Ideas for Teaching Writing as a Process*. Sacramento: California State Department of Education, 1986.

Chapter Two

Dialogue Journals: Personalizing Writing

Probably what most attracts children to diary writing as they are growing up is the secretive aspect of penning something very private, that no one else will see, in a diminutive, special book that contains nothing but the child's thoughts and dreams and personal events. Young children who are in what Piaget would deem the most self-absorbed stage of their lives seem to relish the opportunity to divulge, to no one in particular, all the things about themselves that perhaps no one else is really interested in. Most of us fondly remember some such self-indulgent, whimsical writing.

Until recently, there was no place for such intimate writing in school, leaving a rather large void in the writing curriculum. There has always been a time for children to engage in intimate oral communication with significant people in their lives, in school and out. But writing in school, somehow, has usually been a much more formidable task, mainly concerned with the external, observable form that the writing takes—its vocabulary, grammar, handwriting, and other issues of mechanics—rather than its function, or personal meaning to the child.

Fortunately, today's schools are experiencing a most welcome trend toward "journal writing" that is emerging to fill this need for a personal use of written language and provides much real writing practice as well. The use of a personal journal kept by each child with an allotted time set aside just for the sheer joy of writing is a step forward, to be sure, but the implementation of such writing components is taking many forms, some more beneficial to children than others.

Of the variety of journal-writing formats I have observed being used in elementary classrooms, the one that seems best suited for use in an Affective Language Arts program is the "dialogue journal." The "dialogue" part simply means that in this journal, a running dialogue is on between two people—the teacher and the child. The child begins by writing down anything that is of interest to him or her, and the teacher simply responds by commenting on the child's ideas, asking thoughtful questions, or sometimes merely paraphrasing what the child has said to affirm those thoughts. The teacher, and no one else (unless the child initiates sharing with someone else) reads the entries the child has written.

This chapter will explore some of the important issues involved in starting a dialogue journal writing component of an Affective Language Arts program. Such issues include: 1) What should the children write about? 2) How much should children write? 3) When should they write? 4) How should journal writing be evaluated? 5) What is the rationale for spending valuable curriculum time on such informal writing? While there are many different ways to answer such questions, all equally valid, we will focus here on each of these concerns in terms of how best to provide experiences that foster a real love for writing as an ideal avenue for personal self-expression.

What Should the Children Write About?

I have seen many classrooms in which the question "What shall I write in my journal?" was answered by the teacher assigning a daily topic that the children were instructed to address in their journals that day. While this is certainly a well-meaning technique to get children started, "options" are the real key to success in an Affective Language Arts program. To initially launch the idea of dialogue journals, it might be helpful, instead, to write two or three questions on the blackboard, such as "If you could have any animal that you wanted as a pet, what would you choose? Why?" and "What are some of your favorite things to do on a Saturday morning?" Advising children that these questions are **only** possibilities for writing topics—not "mandates"—then frees those children who already have their own agenda to pursue their own ideas. Note, also, that the topics suggested here were real questions that would require personal, open-ended answers. Too often children are coerced into making their journals outlets for fictional "story" types of pieces, which is all right, as long as it is the child's own wish to use such a genre. My concern is that there is usually plenty of story writing already in the curriculum, so the journal should instead be a possible vehicle through which children could write their personal, first-person statements and vent their feelings and views on life.

An additional possibility for getting the routine of journal writing started is to brainstorm, as a class, at the beginning of the first few writing sessions. During the brainstorming, the teacher might ask the class to decide upon a particular topic, such as music. The teacher would then ask the children to tell what words or phrases come to their minds when they think about music. Since there is no right or wrong answer, children may come up with all sorts of responses that this stimulus provokes. The teacher, then, may choose to "cluster" the responses to help the children mentally organize all the ways it is possible to think about music. For example:

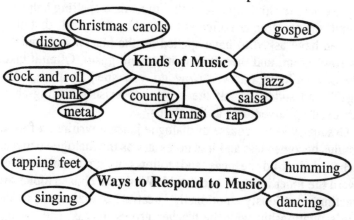

The children might go off into two or three tangents (usually, many more!) in response to the broad term "music." As one student responds "Rock 'n' Roll!" and another pipes up, "Christmas carols!" the teacher then clusters these two similar ideas together, as shown above, under the category "kinds of music," and then performs the same task for "ways we respond to music." With this rudimentary kind of brainstorming about a subject chosen by the class, every child has a chance to respond with his or her own "free association" to the subject, and all the children have begun mentally conjuring up all the different things they know about the topic. Then, keyed in to many possible ideas they could express about the subject, children can write about that topic, assisted by all the ideas on the blackboard, or feel free to pursue their thoughts on something entirely different.

For beginning writers who are often feeling constrained by lack of words that they know how to spell it is often helpful for the teacher to position herself at the blackboard during the entire journal writing session, with the offer that she is there to write down any words that the children might want to spell, but don't know how. The results of this spelling assistance by the teacher are twofold: first, the children are freed to write down whatever they are able to think up due to the immediate spelling help; and second, the children are often stimulated by the words that other children have asked to have spelled on the blackboard, quickly "borrow" them, and then start writing with gusto. Often it takes only one child to query, "How do you spell 'trapeze,' Mr. Vega?" and suddenly half the class is feverishly writing about their exciting adventures at the circus.

Gradually in the course of dialogue journal writing, a formal stimulus becomes less and less necessary as the dialogue between teacher and child deepens and follows its own unique path toward the inner being of each child. While the chosen topics are sometimes cautiously emotionally "neutral" to start with, as the child's relationship with the teacher grows in trust and caring, the child typically begins to grow even closer to the teacher through the writing. A bonding occurs that is intensified through the open communication afforded by the personal, conversational nature of the journal. A child who began her journal with "safe" topics, like her trip to Grandma's or what she likes to eat for breakfast, may begin to use the journal to ask the teacher personal questions such as "Do you have any children, Mrs. Roma?" or "Do you think my new haircut looks dumb?" At this point, when events happen in class that may be unsettling to a child, that child may begin to vent his anger through the journal. He may now use the journal to apologize to the teacher for something he did in class that he wishes he hadn't done, or he may begin to confide in the teacher about hurtful things happening to him at home or in his relationship with others at school. Some children may complain about homework in the journal; others use the journal to confess to "petty crimes" they have committed, such as having told a lie or having cheated on a test, or having taken something that did not belong to them. Too, children begin to use the journal to express feelings that are too embarrassing for them to own up to in person; in writing, they suddenly may feel free to offer their undying love and appreciation for their teacher.

How Much Should Children Write?

Exactly how much writing should be done in the journal on a daily basis is an issue that must be confronted, because it will surface almost immediately (especially with older children who are more entrenched in "the system") and will almost certainly get in the way if not laid to rest. Too often children are instructed to... "write a 250 word essay on ..." or "...write a five page story which tells..." and the more fretful and hesitant writers get so caught up in counting words and pages they soon lose sight of anything they had to say. To avoid this squelching of the free flow of ideas I suggest, instead, that the teacher tell the children at the onset of the dialogue journal writing sessions that during each session **something** must be written, but that the amount is of little significance. Students may write in response to the questions placed on the board, they may take off on the brainstorming topic, or they may even write down the lyrics to a song on the radio that they liked and tell why. In some cases, they may resort to writing down, "I don't know what to write" and then try to explain how they feel about having to write when they feel they have nothing to say! Although the first several entries from the "word counter" will probably be slim pickings, the teacher who waits out the drought will soon be rewarded: as children begin to realize they are really free to write about whatever interests them; when they see that their lack of perfect mechanical prowess in the language is not pointed out; and when they begin to understand that everything that they say will get a thoughtful response from their teacher, I can testify to the fact that they will start writing. They may not become prolific writers in "three easy weeks," but the difference in the quantity and quality of writing produced by erstwhile reluctant writers after several months of using dialogue journals is often striking.

Ideally, children should have time set aside to write in their journals every day. It might commence as a ten minute writing block for primary children and turn into half hour sessions after several months, when children begin finding more and more to say, and look increasingly forward to reading the teacher's responses. Some children may ask to bring their journals home in order to write more in the evening as well; this is a sure sign of success and should be encouraged (but not forced) by all means. For some children with difficult home lives, the journal becomes an outlet for them to react to confusing things that may be happening to them; a sympathetic ear, or in extreme cases, a life-line.

How Should Journal Writing Be Evaluated?

The teacher's responsibility in the dialogue journal is pivotal—and time-consuming; there seems to be no easy way to make the task of writing personal responses less demanding on one's time. However, the tedious, "nitpicky" ordeal of correcting every misspelled word or sentence fragment in red pen is scrupulously avoided here. But the teacher must still read everything each child has written and make appropriate comments as deemed necessary. As the writing progresses, the teacher may be more familiar with the nature of each child's writing; several pages may need no comments or an occasional "What an interesting thought!" or "I agree!" Corrections, in the traditional sense, are **not** made, but the teacher does model, through her paraphrasing or questions, correct form in writing.

The following is an excerpt from the journal of a third-grader in which the process of teacher-modeling, as well as some basic problem-solving, has taken place:

When I grow up I have disided to be a scubba divver. I think it would be so net to swim around with all those fish. Have you ever been scubba divving, Mrs. Reed. You know what Mrs. Reed yesterday in math you said I was talking but it wasn't me. It was Lisa. She is always bothering me Mrs. Reed. Can you change are seats?

How exciting that you have decided to become a scuba diver! No, I have never been scuba diving, Ann. Will you go scuba diving when you go to Florida on vacation? I will see about changing your seat, Ann. I am so sorry you were bothered!

● ● ● ● ●

Yes Mrs. Reed, we are going to go scuba diving when we go to Florida Dad said. I can't wait!! Daddy said we might see some very big and colorfull fish.

In this entry, Ann has spontaneously expressed her current desire to be a "scubba divver" when she grows up. Note that the teacher sensitively responds only to the ideas Ann has, yet in her response, the teacher correctly respells "scuba diver," "decided," "diving" and models the correct punctuation for addressing someone. Note, too, that this is duly noted by the child, who does not feel at all chastised by this "subliminal" correction, but she does spell "scuba diving" correctly in her next use of the words, because it is axiomatic that every child would love to spell everything correctly, if it were just possible for them to know how to spell each word as they needed it.

Also in this entry (practically in the same breath in which she has rhapsodized about becoming a scuba diver!), Ann airs her hurt feelings about a minor altercation that occurred the previous day. While not actually taking Ann's side in the matter, the teacher assents to resolving the problem by separating the two children. The teacher's judgment in originally telling Ann to stop talking may or may not have been in error, but in a typical class of nearly thirty children, many hasty judgment calls must be made. The added perspective offered to the teacher by the dialogue journals is often invaluable.

To make the task of looking over the journals less formidable, some teachers elect to read half the journals every week. This means that all children get feedback on their entries at least every two weeks, yet the teacher's reading and responding is minimized. Often a teacher can respond sensitively to thirteen or fourteen journals within a couple of hours. To be sure, two hours a week is a hefty commitment, but the teacher's rewards in terms of seeing his students' writing become much more fluent cannot be overestimated.

Why Implement Dialogue Journal Writing?
The justification for adding dialogue journal writing to an already overloaded language arts curriculum are many, and in this age of teacher accountability, it would seem they are worth reiterating here. First of all, the improvement in attitude toward

writing of children who have participated in such a program is phenomenal. As was previously mentioned, if the sessions are frequent enough (preferably once a day) and endure for the better part of a school year and include the kind of positive feedback described in this chapter, children at every grade level will be much more favorably inclined toward writing, and will write MORE.

Second, the confidence of children will increase as they begin to believe in their own writing ability and they look **forward** to the teacher's comments rather than dreading the more typical "sea of red marks." As they realize, through their teacher's comments, that their thoughts and ideas have merit, their self-concept, too, will improve. The "nonthreatening" nature of such journals makes them particularly appealing for learners for whom English is a second language. Such learners are often fearful of being publicly ridiculed for their lack of fluency with the language or their misunderstanding of mainstream customs (Peyton and Reed, 1990).

Third, children receive important writing practice through journals and, as a result, they become more fluent writers. As in skiing, typing, or riding a bicycle, writing improves with concerted practice. Moreover, due to the modeling the teacher does, and the prodding questions that he asks, children begin to learn just what kinds of details to elaborate upon in order to make their writing effective. Additionally, through the modeling, children's spelling and other use of mechanics of our language improves markedly. The teacher is able to be there for every child's "teachable moment" of wanting to know how to spell a certain word or how to use an unfamiliar grammatical construct.

Fourth, children begin to see a new use of writing for their own purposes, rather than just completing a teacher-directed assignment. Many children begin to find that writing can be a very cathartic experience—especially when they are venting some very intense feelings and emotions. They often find, too, that writing is a great outlet offering them a way to diffuse potentially explosive situations ahead of time by being able to examine their feelings objectively **before** they act.

Finally, the effect that dialogue journal writing can have on the relationship between teacher and students is perhaps the happiest side benefit of this writing activity. With an affective teacher who does not take lightly the trust of her pupils, the dialogues can lead to a much deeper, holistic understanding of the children that she teaches as distinct individuals. As intimate details of the child's life are offered to a teacher, and that child, in return, is assured that he is indeed a valuable and worthwhile human being, a serendipitous bonding occurs that, under normal over-crowded classroom circumstances would have taken years to build. Additionally, the teacher receives some valuable feedback into the "grapevine" of the classroom culture that a teacher is not ordinarily privy to. She gets some interesting feedback about her teaching techniques, her relationship with pupils, and her handling of classroom crises as they arise. With the privilege of being able to "feel the classroom pulse," if there are any major class concerns, the teacher is one of the first to know.

Summary

The use of the dialogue journal in an Affective Language Arts program is an ideal way to ensure that children receive adequate practice in the kind of intimate, informal practice that is most meaningful to them. The journals can be the prime vehicle through which a capable teacher can gently model effective writing techniques, as well as the mechanics of our language. Such a teacher can also prod children into elaborating on what they themselves have already decided to write about. Although the journals require a commitment of time and effort on the teacher's part, their use tends to produce a greater bonding between teacher and students, and the teacher is able to get a child's-eye-view of the emotional climate of the classroom. Most of all, students who keep dialogue journals grow more confident in their ability to use written communication. With the guidance of a sensitive and affective teacher, children experience the joy of being able to express their innermost thoughts and ideas to a caring adult. Indeed, the highlight of the students' week becomes the moment when their journals are returned by their teacher, and they reread their entries with the teacher's comments to see how their youthful musings were received.

Soon the prosaic "How much do I have to write?" dies a natural death, as the young writers move on to more important questions.

References

Danielson, K.E. *Dialogue Journals: Writing as Conversation.* Bloomington, IN: Phi Delta Kappa Educational Foundation, 1988.

Gambrel, L.B. "Dialogue Journals: Reading-Writing Interaction." *The Reading Teachers* 38 (1985): pp. 512-15.

Kreeft, J. "Dialogue Writing: Bridge from Talk to Essay Writing." *Language Arts* 61 (1984): pp. 141-50.

Lindfors, J.W. "From 'Talking Together' to 'Being Together in Talk'." *Language Arts* 65, No. 2 (February 1988): pp. 135-41.

Peyton, J.K., and L. Reed. *Dialogue Journal Writing with Nonnative English Speakers: A Handbook for Teachers.* Alexandria, VA: Teachers of English to Speakers of Other Languages, 1990.

Staton, J. "Writing and Counseling: Using a Dialogue Journal." *Language Arts* 57 (1980): pp. 514-18.

Staton, J., R. Shay, J. Kreeft, and L. Reed. *Dialogue Journal Communication: Classroom, Linguistic, Social, and Cognitive Views.* Norwood, NJ: Ablex, 1987.

Chapter Three

Copy-Cat Books:
Expanding Upon Children's Literature

Mrs. Perry has just finished reading "The Three Billy Goats Gruff" to her second graders. The story is one they have heard before, and because this is so, they know what is coming and eagerly chime in, "Trip, trap, trip, trap!" at the appropriate times and spontaneously cheer and applaud when the ugly troll is sent flying over the bridge. Now Mrs. Perry has an irresistible proposition for the children: "Let's write a new story much like this one, only we can change the characters. What three animals could we have who need to get somewhere?" The class decides upon three dinosaurs—a big one, a small one, and an in-between one. She then asks her charges, "Where might the dinosaurs be heading in our new story?" Enrique offers that the dinosaurs might be on their way to the jungle to find some ferns, as these dinosaurs are of the plant eating variety. "Who or what might stop our dinosaurs from getting to the jungle?" Mrs. Perry inquires. Lorena insists that they must swim across a deep lake, but there is a huge monster in the lake, not unlike the Loch Ness monster that she has read about. Her contribution is greeted with much appreciation and excitement; these second-graders are quite fond of monsters. The class is ready to compose. As they take turns thinking up new lines for a modified story, Mrs. Perry transcribes their ideas onto the blackboard. The children will copy their new story, and some children will be inspired to write yet another new version of "The Billy Goats Gruff" on their own. Meanwhile, Graciela, the class artist, has drawn the dinosaur family, the Loch Ness monster, a lake, and a jungle to use with the flannel board so that the class can later retell their new story, *Three Dinosaurs Daring* with the help of her felt cut-outs.

This teacher has demonstrated how certain literature can be successfully used to inspire children to adapt the existing rhyme schemes, ideas, or catchy phrases of stories they know and love. We know that great artists and writers of the past have often begun their careers by first modeling the products of esteemed artists and writers; it seems only fitting that children should be given similar opportunities to learn some techniques from the masters of children's literature. This "copy-catting" method not only reinforces the children's appreciation for the literature, but it also gradually encourages them to become authors by providing them with a tried-and-true structure that they already know will be wonderful.

The remainder of this chapter will describe how ten favorite children's books can be read to a class and then turned into new creations by allowing children to copy some part of the book. While this is only a small sample, Appendix I contains many other books that have patterns that also lend themselves to similar modeling. Hopefully, the affective teacher reading this book can soon follow many read-aloud sessions by encouraging his students to write new books.

A House Is a House For Me

Mary Ann Hoberman's enchanting book takes children from reality to fantasy while having them consider just what constitutes the concept of a "house." She starts out with obvious enough statements: "A web is a house for a spider; A coop? That's a house for a chicken," and always comes back to the phrase..."and a house is a house for me." Later in the book, however, the author begins to be more broad in her interpretation of what a "house" can be, and the fun begins. "A sandwich is home for some ham...a throat is a house for a hum ...a mirror's a house for reflections." Children delight in these far-fetched ideas and are then ready to write a new book of their own with some original ideas that may not have been included in Hoberman's book. For additional inspiration, one class leafed through magazines, and then came up with a wonderfully imaginative book. Here's an excerpt:

A radio is a house for music,
The sky is a house for a rainbow,
Heaven is home to the angels,
And a house is a house for me.

A chest is a house for a cough,
A blizzard is a house for a snowman,
A cup is a home for chicken noodle soup,
And a house is a house for me.

What Do You Say, Dear?

What Do You Say, Dear? is a wonderfully tongue-in-cheek compilation of episodes in which children find themselves in rather unusual circumstances that require them to consider their repertoire of courteous phrases and select just the right one. Each episode ends with the query, "What do you say, dear?" For example, my favorite: "You have gone downtown to do some shopping. You are walking backwards because sometimes you like to, and you bump into a crocodile. What do you say, dear? —Excuse me." After the eleven hilarious episodes in the book have been read to the class, children are tuned in to the author's sense of humor and are ready to write an "etiquette" book of their own. It is helpful to first write a list of the possible courteous phrases on the blackboard or overhead. Then, after the whole class has helped to brainstorm one or two far-fetched situations that would require such courteous phrases, children can be broken up into small groups, with each group responsible for two or three more phrases. For example, one group came up with these episodes:

You are swimming in the ocean when suddenly
a great white shark appears and is about to
chomp on your leg. Suddenly a skin diver

appears and spears the shark. What do you say, dear?—Thank you very much.

Bon Jovi is putting on a rock concert in your bedroom. Your mother is trying to whisper something in your ear but you can't quite hear her. What do you say, dear?—I beg your pardon?

If It Weren't For You

Charlotte Zolotow has written several books with wistful, recurring phrases with which every child can readily identify. *If It Weren't For You* is one such book. In Zolotow's story, a young boy is reflecting upon all the things that would be possible if it weren't for his little brother: "If it weren't for you I'd be an only child and I'd get all the presents. I could have the whole last slice of cake and the biggest piece of candy in the box." The child does finally concede, however, that if it weren't for his little brother..."I'd have to be alone with the grown-ups." Children who may not have siblings still may have similar ambivalent feelings about many people—even their parents and teacher. To use the motif of the book requires that first the whole class brainstorms some people about whom they sometimes have mixed feelings. Discuss the fact that this is true in **any** relationship; people we love can often cause us problems! Start off with the phrase "If it weren't for you..." and let the class express some resentments. For a final line let them think of some positive element that the person adds to their lives (the old "bait and switch"!) to end the story on a happy note. One class devised these lines about their teacher:

If it weren't for you, Mrs. Sowa,
I wouldn't have to wake up on a Monday morning,
I wouldn't have to do any homework.
I wouldn't have to stay in at recess when I've been rude.
If it weren't for you, I'd be fishing right now!

But it's also true, if it weren't for you,
I wouldn't have learned as much as I know now.

Someday

Charlotte Zolotow's earlier book *Someday* has a motif of a
day far in the future when the things that go predictably wrong
will all of a sudden be perfect—the stuff of dreams. Every child
can relate to this child's "Someday I'm going to dancing class
and Miss Bird will say, 'Ellen is doing it just right. Everybody
watch her,' or 'Someday I'm going to catch a high, high ball and
my team will win because I did it.'" For children to adapt this
book into their own wistful "someday" projections, a
brainstorming session should begin with sharing some everyday
experiences that children have had that are usually quite
frustrating. "Someday" perhaps these situations could be
reversed, as these fifth-graders wrote:

> Someday I'm going to make blueberry pancakes
> and flip them high in the air and they will land
> just in the right place on the griddle—NOT on
> the floor!

> Someday my big brother will say to me, "Was
> there something you would prefer to watch on
> TV rather than football? I would be happy to
> change the channel for you!"

Rosie's Walk

Pat Hutchins has written a book for very young children
that establishes a simple pattern of prepositional phrases that
children can have fun duplicating using their own walk—real or
imaginary—as a guide. *Rosie's Walk* takes Rosie, the hen, on a
walk "...across the yard, around the pond, over the haystack,
...and back in time for dinner." The story can be read aloud to
primary children and then, after a brief recap about all the places
that Rosie went, followed by a walk to the library or around the

school yard, or even an imaginary walk with eyes closed to some far-away place. After a walk and the second reading of the book, children will want to write their own book, using Hutchins' patterns of prepositions, about their walk:

> Mrs. Najera's class went for a walk
> across the field,
> around the swings,
> over the sandbox,
> past the jungle gym,
> through the bushes
> under the slide
> and got back in time for recess.

A variation with older children might include adding descriptive adjectives to each place that was visited. One fourth grade class, for example, wrote:

> Mrs. Nakahira's class went for a walk
> Across the congested auditorium,
> Around the inviting water fountain,
> Over the well-traveled tile,
> Past the deafening lunch room,
> Through the quiet halls,
> Under the acoustic ceiling,
> And got back in time to turn in their math homework!

Animals Should Definitely NOT Wear Clothing

Judi Barrett's book tickles children's funny bones and inspires them to add to her ideas with their own creations. With entries such as "Animals should definitely NOT wear clothing because it could be very messy for a pig," and "...because a giraffe might look sort of silly," with amusing illustrations to match, children are ready to write. Fortunately, Barrett has used nowhere near all the possible animals in her book, so the next step, after reading the book aloud, is to have children brainstorm some other animals not included in the original book and for the teacher to write them on the blackboard or overhead. Next, brainstorm some possible problems that two or three of these animals might have if they were to wear clothing:

> Animals should definitely **not** wear clothing
> ...because a skunk might make them smelly;
> ...because a whale would wet them with his spout;
> ...because a cat could claw them to bits.

After the whole group effort, children can be divided into groups of four or five and given an animal from those just contributed on the blackboard. Each group then brainstorms a possible reason why their animal should **not** wear clothing because... Each group's phrase is then combined with the other groups to make a new class book. Groups can, of course, be encouraged to illustrate their phrases, using Barrett's hilarious drawings as a guideline.

Brown Bear, Brown Bear, What Do You See?
Bill Martin's classic *Brown Bear, Brown Bear* is a favorite with primary children because of its clever rhyming and repetition, and it lends itself to the fresh ideas of children who will like using the same pattern:

> Redbird, redbird, what do you see?
> I see a yellow duck looking at me.
> Yellow duck, yellow duck, what do you see?
> I see a blue horse looking at me.

After the children have listened to this book, they are ready to brainstorm some new creatures or objects to consider what **these** objects might see. The original brainstorming might take place orally, as a group game, after the first object has been decided upon, and might proceed like this:

Candle stick, candle stick,
What do you see?
I see a matchstick
That's going to burn me!
Matchstick, matchstick
What do you see?
I see wind
That's going to blow me.

After this oral "warm up" exercise, an add-on, or cumulative, book can be written by the class. Each child individually selects a creature or object and combines it with the question, "What do you see?" This question is exchanged with another child. Each child answers the other's question with, "I see a (rhyme)." This exercise is repeated nine or ten times, until each child has written several questions and answers and has completed an ending line to one new book.

I Know What I Like

Part of every child's coming to terms with who he is involves sharing his opinions about what he likes and what he doesn't like. As the sum total of these likes and dislikes makes a unique individual so also the sum total of each child's likes and dislikes can create a new book that can be patterned after Norma Simon's *I Know What I Like*. Most of the "likes" in Simon's books are ones that most children will subscribe to: "I like to taste peanut butter...I like to see kittens...I like to be first in line ..." And the dislikes equally popular: "But I don't like to taste this medicine...I don't like to see scary television...I don't like to be spanked."

Simon's book will surely inspire a discussion of likes and dislikes and the inevitable disagreements may give the affective teacher an opportunity to reinforce the idea that there is no "right" or "wrong" when it comes to opinions; it is okay to disagree with one another. The class as a whole can then brainstorm on the blackboard some things that they like to see, hear, taste, be, and try, as in Simon's book, and then, in an opposite column, make a list of some things they do **not** like to see, hear, taste, be, and try. Encourage children to then write their **own** books that describe their own personal likes and dislikes. Additionally, children may be inspired to illustrate their books by looking at Dora Leder's sometimes humorous accompanying pictures.

Alexander and the Terrible, Horrible, No-Good, Very Bad Day

Everyone has an occasional bad day now and then, and Judith Viorst makes light of this subject by introducing Alexander, who is having a day in which absolutely everything is going wrong—from waking up with bubble gum in his hair to having his Mickey Mouse night light burn out. Every unfortunate episode ends with the observation, "It was...a terrible, horrible, no good, very bad day," and children, as always, look forward to this repetitive phrase.

Viorst's book makes a perfect story for a copy-cat book. After reading it and reiterating all the things that went wrong for poor Alexander, children can be asked to tell about some bad days that they have had and what it was that made them that way. They can then write their own story, including their experiences, real or made-up, interspersing every two or three unhappy events with, "It was a terrible, horrible, no good, very bad day."

Conversely, some children may want to talk about a very **good** day they had and tell why. Real or imaginary events can be used to write a book that describes a perfect day. One fourth-grader, for example, decided to pen "Nicole and the Wonderful, Marvelous, Very Good, Exceptionally Fine Day."

Earl's Too Cool for Me

Every child has looked at other children who seem to be smarter and more sophisticated, and felt inferior. They often imagine such "cool" people might not even want to associate with them. Leah Komaiko presents Earl, who is just this sort of amazing person. At the end of the book, however, readers find that Earl is quite friendly and down-to-earth.

Ask children to share a time when they were similarly intimidated by a person's seemingly superior qualities, only to discover that the person was really approachable and not even "perfect." Share the book with the children and point out the format that lends itself to copy-catting:

> Earl's got a bicycle made of hay,
> He takes rides on the Milky Way,
> Earl's too cool for me.

Have the class write a "Too Cool" (or "Too Neat," or "Too Smart," etc.) book on the blackboard. Then ask children to brainstorm some other possible attributes, choose one, and write a copy-cat "Too..." book of their own. An end product might look like this:

> Bob has Jordan Air tennis shoes,
> He plays a saxophone and sings the blues.
> Bob's too fashionable for me.

Summary

Copy-cat books can be an excellent device to extend the positive feelings of a read-aloud experience through a session in which children use some of the same themes, ideas, phrases, or repetitive schemes in a book to write a new text—borrowing some ideas here, adding an original thought there.

In this chapter, ten children's books were selected and sample, teacher-tested ways to use their motifs to create new books were described. While every trade book may not lend itself to this wonderful reading-writing interaction, much of the available literature for young children contains the kind of repetition and predictable phrases that inspire children to write similar stories, or even to forge ahead into different directions.

Appendix I offers a bibliography of many other children's books that can also be used for copy-cat sessions by an affective teacher who wants to show her students just how rewarding it can be to write books—with a little help from some of the masters of children's literature.

References

Barrett, J. *Animals Should Definitely Not Wear Clothing.* New York: Atheneum, 1973.

Cloer, T. *A Teacher's Handbook of Language Experience Activities.* New York: Macmillan, 1990.

Hoberman, M.A. *A House Is a House For Me.* New York: Viking Press, 1978.

Hutchins, P. *Rosie's Walk.* New York: Macmillan, 1968.

Joslyn, S. *What Do You Say, Dear?* New York: Young Scott Books, 1958.

Komaiko, L. *Earl's Too Cool for Me.* Ill. by L. Cornell. New York: Trumpet Club, 1988.

Simon, N. *I Know What I Like.* Chicago: Albert Whitman & Co., 1971.

Viorst, J. *Alexander and the Terrible, Horrible, No Good, Very Bad Day.* New York: Atheneum, 1982.

Wuertenberg, J. "Conferencing With Young Authors." Paper presented at the annual Bill Martin Literacy Conference, East Texas State University, Commerce, TX, 1986.

Zolotow, C. *If It Weren't For You.* New York: Harper & Row, 1966.

_____. *Someday.* New York: Harper & Row, 1965.

Chapter Four

Episodic Novels:
Becoming REAL Authors

If asked to describe one's most pleasant reading experience, most avid readers might immediately conjure up a full-length novel that was devoured recently, or perhaps many years ago. Whether it be an autobiography, a thriller, or a modern romance, there is something special—even endearing—about a multi-chaptered story that an author has carefully crafted with three-dimensional characters created in an exact time and place with a certain set of problems and resolutions. We feel it is a privilege to share the fictional lives of these characters. But it is the very length of a novel, as compared with shorter genres, that allows the reader this greater time of getting to know the characters, and thus makes the reading experience all that much more intense. Moreover, it must be admitted that the sheer volume of pages in most novels gives us a feeling of some satisfaction at having persevered and finished the tome!

As children enter the intermediate grades they, too, start to read lengthier books. Brief picture story books begin to give way to stories divided into chapters with highly sophisticated plots and, as children are reaching the period in their lives when their adult reading interests are formed, they are also introduced to the pleasures of "armchair escapism" that can be found in a protracted literary experience like reading a novel.

Although children at this age are often reading longer books, their writing assignments, while tending to become more complex, are rarely lengthening to a similar degree. Most students in the intermediate grades are still instructed to write short stories, two-page compositions, and 250-word essays, with only an occasional research paper that may stretch beyond the usual succinct expectations. Teachers often complain that they are pulling teeth to get them to write even that much!

But I have found that children who have had the experience of writing an original episodic novel—with several discrete chapters—come away with a much more memorable feeling of accomplishment, and a fair sense of pride at having produced a new set of characters who have evolved with time and effort and have become real to them. Children who write episodic novels are also understandably quite impressed that their creation resembles an "adult" novel in size and scope. I am convinced that no other writing experience can offer children such an overwhelming sense of authorship.

Tried and true ways to help children bridge the gap from composition writers to episodic novelists will be explored in the remainder of this chapter.

Story Maps

To prepare children for the formidable-sounding task of writing a novel, they first need practice identifying the components of fiction—short stories as well as novels. They need to recognize and be able to produce these fictional elements:

• **Character(s)**. The hero or heroine of the story. What does (s)he look like? How old is (s)he? What is his/her personality like? What does (s)he enjoy doing? What has his/her life been like up until now? Would we like him/her?

• **Setting**. Where and when will the story take place? What does the place look like, feel like, smell like, sound like?

• **Episodes** (eventually, chapters). What sequence of events will happen to the main character(s) and how will he or she feel about what happens? Who will the character(s) consult? How will they make decisions? What will they do next?

• **Consequences** (could be after each episode or all episodes). What happens when the character(s) carry out their plans? Do they succeed? What or who gets in their way? How do they feel?

• **Reactions** (ending for novel). What did the main character(s) learn from all these episodes? How is (s)he different from when we first met him/her? What can we learn from all of this?

The above fictional elements should be routinely discussed with children after they have finished reading books individually or as a group. As they become increasingly facile at identifying these components as they encounter them in short stories and novels, it becomes very natural for them to want to create their own.

Brainstorming

To initiate the novel-writing process, it is helpful to see the previously discussed structure to brainstorm some rudimentary novel ideas together as a class. One fourth-grade class produced the following ideas for a novel.

Characters. The hero of the story is a very kind, but timid scientist who keeps botching up his experiments. He has had nothing but bad luck in his life. His wife and children died in an automobile accident and his dog was poisoned. He is very old and bald, skinny and very nervous. He speaks very slowly (he keeps forgetting what he was going to say) and he says "hmmm" a lot.

Setting. Our scientist lives on a small island in the Pacific Ocean sometime in the future. The island is very green and smells like coconuts and salty breezes. The land is uninhabited except for a few natives and sometimes tourists whose ships get wrecked on the island.

Episodes. (chapters)

1) A very evil sailor gets shipwrecked on the island. He wants the island for himself and he is afraid of the natives, so he decides to kill them (he has a gun).

2) The natives decide to go to war against the sailor. They have no weapons except spears. They're not good fighters.

3) The natives lose the war. Many of them are shot and several die. The evil sailor thinks he got rid of them forever, but he didn't. Two are still alive.

4) One of the natives asks the scientist if he will devise a potion that will make the sailor fall asleep so that they can steal his gun.

5) The scientist thinks about it for a long time, but then he says no (he is too shy). The natives are very sad.

6) Then the scientist gets very sick with a tropical disease (malaria). The natives save him by bringing him tea and herbs. He gets better.

7) The scientist is very grateful, because he realizes the natives saved his life. He decides to make the potion.

8) The natives put the potion in the drinking water of the sailor while he is cleaning his gun.

Consequences. The sailor drinks the water and falls asleep. The natives take the gun and bury it under a tree. The sailor wakes up and the natives make peace with him. They shake hands.

Reactions. The scientist decides he has been selfish his whole life and that was probably why he had such bad luck. The sailor makes friends with the scientist and helps him to do his experiments without botching them up.

Moral: If you are kind to people and use your talents wisely, people will want to help you and your luck will get better!

Small Groups

Having brainstormed some rudimentary ideas for the class episodic novel, children are now ready to break into groups of two or three writing partners to elaborate on the ideas that were contributed in the whole group session. The above brainstorming session produced twelve discrete components of the story, which would now be called episodes, or chapters. Each writing team would now select one of these chapter parts and expand the germ that was brainstormed into a more fully developed composition. The writing partners are especially helpful here, because the children can continue to bounce ideas off one another orally, as the inspiration is still fresh from the recent group brainstorming. Also, the children in each writing group can serve as editors to read and reread their group's effort for any glaring spelling or punctuation errors. As all this thinking and writing is going on, the teacher is moving from group to group, listening to each group as they are expounding their ideas to support and affirm, but also to prevent any group from radically deviating from the ideas set forth in another chapter.

Group Conferences
     When each group has finished its episode and turned it in, the teacher calls conferences with each group. First she checks to see that each episode makes a logical transition from one chapter to the next, while keeping all the characters somewhat consistent in their behavior. While maintaining respect for the authors' words and ideas, the teacher may ask the authors to expand an idea or phrase, or advise them of some information they may need from other chapters written by other groups (at this stage, only the teacher is privy to the **whole** novel!). Now is also the optimal time to show each group of children how to make their descriptions more lively and realistic by using dialogue. Children who have not had this instruction will usually create lines such as, "The natives asked the scientist if he would devise a potion to make the sailor fall asleep."
     Children are now open to the idea that the same idea is much more powerful like this:
          "Sir, could you help us by devising a potion that
          would make the sailor fall asleep?" the native
          hopefully inquired.
     The group then prepares a revised chapter.

Sharing the Novel
     Using this abbreviated group writing technique, the class has just written a twelve-chapter novel, and the next step—sharing it—will ensure that each individual author will soon be ready to

branch out on his or her own. With ceremonious acclaim the teacher reads the novel (so as to avoid conflicts between group members as to who should read their chapter), as well as to provide the appropriate savoir-faire!

After plenty of congratulatory behavior all around, the children can be asked to write their final finished copy with one illustration contributed by each author. Then the final product can be shared with others outside the classroom, as discussed in chapter two, and used as an inspiration for future episodic novels.

The Individually-Written Novel

After the intensive group exercise in novel writing, most children feel confident enough to attempt to write a novel of their own, while looking forward to a product that is as exciting, yet expedient, as the group effort was. Of course, the individual effort will take much longer, but the children must be reminded that the more chapters they add to their novel, the more interesting and fun it will be to write.

The teacher then provides an extensive episodic outline for each child. This outline differs from the story maps only in that specific chapter ideas are offered in episodic-size chunks. Also, outlines might focus on themes of a certain emotion, such as grief, envy, hatred, love, or hope. Or, after reading a wide variety of Greek or Roman myths, children can pick a similar hero or heroine. Using the basic story elements already described, the writer can have the hero and his actions try to explain the creation of one of our natural phenomena, such as floods, tornadoes, lightning, etc.

Because children have already had some experience with the previous shared novel in character development, as well as the need for a setting, problems, and resolution, these particular facets are woven into the novel outline, which can become increasingly complex as the children start to demand more sophisticated plots. The following is a simple episodic novel outline that works well with intermediate age children who have already had some practice writing shared episodic novels. It can be expanded as needed:

Chapter One: Invent and describe a character. Is (s)he real or pretend? What does (s)he look like? Where does (s)he live? How does (s)he behave? What things does (s)he like to do? What things are special about him/her?

Chapter Two: What is your character's family like? Describe his/her friends. Tell about some things that may have happened to him/her when (s)he was a baby and growing up.

Chapter Three: Describe one full day in the life of your character. Does (s)he work or go to school? Where and what does (s)he like to play? Who and what does (s)he play with? What does (s)he eat? What kinds of things usually happen?

Chapter Four: Your character is going on a trip. How does (s)he decide to go on this trip? How does (s)he prepare for it? How does (s)he feel about going?

Chapter Five: Just before going on the trip, someone warns your character not to go on this trip. Who or what warns your character? Should your character go? Why or why not? Describe your character's thoughts and feelings now.

Chapter Six: Your character decides to go on the trip anyway. What makes him/her decide? Describe your character's voyage there and his/her feelings on the way.

Chapter Seven: Your character has a wonderful, magical first day at his/her destination. Describe the place at which your character has arrived. Tell what made the first day so extra special.

Chapter Eight: The second day of the trip your character meets someone or something very strange. Who or what? Describe what makes this person so strange and tell about what happens at the meeting.

Chapter Nine: The strange person [or thing] asks your character to do something evil, but your character doesn't want to. The strange person says something bad will happen if your character doesn't do the evil thing. Describe the bad thing and the conversation between your character and the strange person.

Tell what is supposed to happen if your character does not do what is asked of him/her.

Chapter Ten: Your character decides not to do the evil thing. Describe how (s)he reaches this decision. Your character then decides to go home early from the trip to try to escape from the strange person and the bad things that will happen. Describe his/her escape.

Chapter Eleven: The strange person spies your character just as (s)he is about to leave. The strange person chases your character all over the city. Describe the chase.

Chapter Twelve: Your character gets away from the strange person just in time and arrives home safely. Tell about your character's feelings. What did (s)he learn from the problem with the strange person? What did (s)he learn about him/herself? What is your character thinking and feeling as we leave him/her?

To initiate the writing of this individually composed episodic novel, it is helpful to introduce the outline for one episode at a time and then to brainstorm a myriad of ideas with the whole class. This time, instead of trying to develop a group composite novel, the teacher is trying to elicit as many ideas as possible, so that children can be inspired to select an idea to work up by themselves. For example, in the first episode the characters brainstormed as a class may range from a telepathic Martian to a foxy lady living out on the prairie with eight children. Most importantly, it is crucial to underscore the fact that there are no right or wrong characters here; just a great many ideas to share, each of which could be the start of an interesting novel.

After the class brainstorming session, each child selects a character that has been mentioned, or one that they have thought of but hadn't shared, and then they flesh out the chapter outline with class ideas as well as their own. Children can then be paired up with an editing partner to read each other's chapter, do some initial editing, and make some POSITIVE responses, as well as requests for more information ("Can you tell me more about what happened when the angel broke her leg?").

Novel writing sessions are usually about a week apart, with revisions and teacher conferences in between. By the second session, children are enjoying getting a chance to tell even more about their character. Now, because each child has his/her individual character in mind, the class brainstorming becomes less and less important and serves more as a general prompt to writing. When children are following the outline just discussed, they very often like to offer anecdotes that were shared by their family about **their** infancy and sometimes they are incorporated into the second chapter of their novel (novels **are** often thinly-veiled autobiographies, we are told!).

By the third session, most children are usually feeling very close to their characters and are looking forward to expanding them. The teacher's job at this point is to go around to individual children who are temporarily "blocked" and affirm ideas that they come up with, urging them to relax, close their eyes, and trust their own "mind pictures."

By the fourth session, the characters in most novels have usually evolved to the point where they have lives of their own. Therefore, as the teacher introduces the chapter outline, she can encourage children to feel free to deviate from the outline if they feel their own characters are quite naturally heading in other directions. As more and more episodes are written, the outline becomes less and less important, and the bulk of ideas that have already been established becomes the positive impetus that makes children excited about working on their novels.

When the last chapter has been completed through the joint efforts of the child, the teacher, and the editorial partner (with twelve chapters, this usually takes about three months), children are actually eager to do the illustrating and laborious final editing. A title is chosen with great care, to catch the reader's attention and also to capture what the novel is mainly about. Finished novels are worthy of professional plastic ring binding, which can often be done by the media center or a PTA looking for worthwhile projects. As the final products are completed, the teacher reads them to the class during read aloud time, instead of the usual fare of children's literature, yet with the same attention to author, illustrator and preliminary predictions as to what the children think the story will be about and what they think the main character might do next. After such an extreme effort, each author's moment in the read-aloud spotlight is enough to bolster his feelings about himself as a budding author of novels, perhaps forever.

Summary

Although children enjoy reading and listening to longer stories as they reach the intermediate grades, there are often few opportunities for them to experience writing anything as lengthy and involved as a novel. By having children first become familiar with the elements in a longer story, or a novel, the teacher can help them to break down the project into smaller components that may seem less threatening and more possible for them. Brainstorming some rudimentary ideas for each story part and then assigning each part to a group is an ideal way to launch the idea of novel writing, as children quickly get to see the finished whole group project and are very proud of what they have contributed to. They are then ready, with the help of an action-promising episodic novel outline, to write their own individual novels. The teacher introduces one chapter idea for each weekly session and after some class brainstorming, allows children to proceed on their own. As the sessions go along and the characters evolve, children begin to feel very close to their creations and look forward to adding new dimensions to their characters' lives. Often, the teacher's outline becomes obsolete as the spunky characters take off on their own journeys from each child's vivid imagination.

As the novels are completed, they are read by the teacher with gusto, just as she would read any children's novel during read-aloud time. In the child's perspective, it has been a long, long time from the start of the novel to its finish, but suddenly it is all worthwhile and she is already thinking about the next one.

Chapter Five

Other Motivators:
When They Don't Know What to Write

The mere presence of a blank sheet of paper causes Dana to begin writing furiously, penning her elaborate fantasies or scary whodunits with elan. On the other hand, Yolanda, in the same classroom, stubbornly resists writing and constantly complains to her teacher, "But I don't know what to write!" The harried teacher, tired of the plaintive little phrase, rationalizes that she, the teacher, could not be to blame if the Yolandas in her class do not write eagerly, for the prolific Danas are there to attest to the teacher's expertise as writing motivator—or so she would like to believe. Most affective teachers, however, are not satisfied until EVERY child is feeling joyful success at communicating his or her thoughts and ideas in written form.

Yet the sad lament, "I don't know what to write!" is too familiar in most classrooms, with some children. The goal, therefore, is always to spark that zest for writing not just in some, but in ALL children. Achieving this goal consists, in part, of piquing the imagination of children by providing exciting writing activities that they feel confident they can do because they have first participated in a group brainstorming effort. More importantly, achieving this goal also centers around providing a fertile classroom atmosphere that is most conducive to fostering creativity. By the term "creativity" what is meant here is not the usually proffered pedagogical definition: "a piece of writing that is original, clever," or simply "cute"; creativity is defined by this author in a broader sense, and includes a whole compendium of ways that children might freely express themselves, by way of a socially sensitive observation, a well-constructed practical joke, or a reflective question, for example, as well as the more traditional means of demonstrating creativity via the production of an aesthetically pleasing work of art. Just how broadly creativity is defined by the affective teacher is crucial, because far too often creative ideas are unnoticed, or worse yet, actively squelched because well-meaning teachers are adhering to an unnecessarily rigid definition of the term; for the good news is that research suggests that creativity is not necessarily inherited, but can actually be developed in the right kind of environment. If this is so, affective teachers must be committed to the notion that ALL children can be encouraged to express ideas, words, and concepts that are the personal products of their own unique experiences and fertile imaginations; every child CAN have the emotional luxury of a creative outlet.

The remainder of this chapter will include some important axioms for nurturing creativity in the classroom, and will also provide some teacher-tested ways to actively inspire creative expression for even the most reluctant of would-be writers.

Fostering Creativity in the Classroom

A researcher interested in exploring the nature of creativity once did an experiment involving a "test" of creativity. He showed several children a rock and gave them these instructions: "I want you to think of as many things as you can that could be done with this rock." To a similar group of six children he gave these slightly different instructions: "I want you to think of as many clever and unusual things as you can to do with this rock. Only think of very 'good' ideas." The results of this researcher's study, as you may have guessed, showed that the children who were not restricted and made intellectually self-conscious by having to continually monitor the quality of their ideas, the first group, came up with significantly more things to do with the rock than the other group. And, ironically, their ideas were more imaginative and original—or "creative." The study makes an important observation about what is most needed to foster creativity in the classroom: There must be a lack of self-consciousness, and children must feel free to create, without anxiety about how others might perceive their product.

Following are suggestions for providing the kind of classroom environment that is most conducive to nurturing creativity in the classroom.

• **Value what is unique about each child.** Although the large number of children in most elementary classrooms makes a certain amount of group conformity necessary, the affective teacher will always make it his business to find out what is truly special about each child. He will make it clear that he values a child's personal statement, whether it is expressed through an unusual hairstyle, an interesting manner of speech, or a unique way of looking at the world.

• **Constantly stress that there is more than one answer to most important questions.** Because the rudimentary components of learning (for example, times tables) are so often on a factual or memorization level, children may unfortunately begin to believe that there is a "correct" answer to everything—even a correct way to write out their own fantasies. Children must feel free to risk exploring alternative solutions to problems and feel comfortable considering other different ways of looking at the world. An affective teacher can foster this approach by frequently asking, "Does anyone else have a **different** idea about that?" or "Is there another way we could think about this?" while affirming a variety of thoughtful responses.

• **Ask many questions requiring critical thinking and provide adequate "think time."** An atmosphere where creativity is nurtured is also one in which children are continually stretched beyond simple "yes" and "no" answers to questions. They are provoked to think about the teacher's questions, as well as those of their classmates. The affective teacher must be comfortable with moments of silence that give each child the opportunity to carefully reflect upon why they feel the way they do.

• **Model creativity for your students in whatever way you can.** Most teachers that I have observed possess some sort of creative talents (especially if one allows a broad definition of the term), but teachers can be unduly modest. All creative aptitudes should be proudly displayed in the classroom! If, on the other hand, one is truly **not** creative, an avid appreciation for creativity when it is manifested in colleagues, world and national figures, as well as the students, will compensate.

• **Never assign grades to creative work.** Assigning letter or numerical grades to any piece of personal authorship, especially if the grade is less than satisfactory, is one of the surest ways to thwart all future creative attempts of reluctant writers. Besides the obvious argument that art is "subjective" and cannot be absolutely evaluated, there is the deeper concern that a low grade on a child's proud work may be profoundly harmful to that child's concept of himself as creator. Thoughtful comments that address the ideas that the author is trying to express are preferable, and the teacher's words are graciously received by the children.

• **When sharing written work, never single out some as "the best" and (heaven forbid) "the worst."** Again, yours is a single subjective evaluation, and children must be allowed to create in the manner that their own heart, soul, and imagination dictate. It is far better to point out some strengths in **all** pieces of writing that are read aloud and to help children learn to critically evaluate their own writing.

• **Incorporate creativity into the TOTAL program.** Creativity is sadly diminished as an entity when it is encouraged and expected only at certain specified times, such as in "creative writing time," or during art, music, and language arts. An affective teacher must believe in, and model, creative approaches to math, science and everything else in the curriculum—even a layup shot in basketball could have its creative aspect. To really free children, creativity must be encouraged and integrated into **every** phase of the school day.

Tried and True Activities to Inspire Creative Writing

Even the most reluctant writers can be motivated to write if they are given a bit of a boost initially, either through a fixed writing formula, a provocative idea, or an outright "gimmick." The following ideas contain one or more of these elements, and have been used often with young writers who just have a difficult time getting started. Many practicing teachers I have worked with have proclaimed these motivators to be "just what the doctor ordered" to get the pencils burning.

• **Dear Abby.** Carefully select from an advice column some letters that pose problems that would be of interest to your class. Read several of them to the children and have them brainstorm some possible solutions to the problems that have been posed by the writers. Here is an example of the kind of letters that children cannot resist responding to:

Dear Abby,
The question I want to ask is so indelicate I am having trouble putting it down on paper. Please tell me how to let a very nice gentleman know it is improper to blow one's nose at the table in a linen napkin. I don't mean wipe, Abby; I mean **honk**.
—Nameless

After children have orally brainstormed some possible solutions to the dilemma of "Nameless," read Abby's answer:

Dear Nameless,
The next time the 'gentleman' honks, ask him if he has a handkerchief. Then explain what it is for.

The chances are excellent that your students will have come up with a solution just as good, if not better, than Abby's.

Next, read two or three other letters of concern and let children select one for which they will write individual responses.

Finally, have children divide up into partners. Encourage each child to write a letter describing a problem, real or fictitious, which solicits a solution. Then let partners exchange letters and try to solve the problem of their partners, "Dear Abby" style (for grades 4-6).

• **Animal Crackers.** Place an animal cracker on the desk of each child with instructions to look at and think about the animal, but don't eat it. Make a list on the blackboard or overhead of all the animals that are represented in the room and

ask for words that describe each animal, and facts the children
know about each one. Then, returning attention to the animal
crackers on each desk, discuss the following questions:

Are these animals alive?

How do you think the animal felt about being in the box?

How does it feel to be out of the box?

What might your animal say right now if it could talk?

Does your animal miss its friends from the box?

What does your animal eat?

Does your animal know it will soon be eaten?

How does it feel about that?

Finally, have the children write a story about their animal
using the discussion questions, facts, and descriptive words on
the board to help them. When they are finished, allow them to
eat their cracker, although some may choose to keep it as a
"pet"! (Grades 1-3.)

• **Story Plots**. Introduce this activity as a "Mystery Story-
Telling" project. Have the children select three numbers, each
ranging between one and twelve (for example, 4, 3, and 11).
The numbers will serve to identify pre-determined parts of the
story, as listed below:

Character	Event	Result
1. lonesome witch	1. became invisible	1. was put in jail
2. rich hobo	2. learned to speak Chinese	2. left the country
3. mysterious taxi driver	3. discovered a new planet	3. got rich
4. toothless tiger	4. hated the sun	4. received an award
5. evil cowboy	5. got stuck in an elevator	5. got picture in paper
6. forgetful astronaut	6. got the hiccups	6. caused an earthquake
7. bashful girl	7. fell in a deep hole	7. lost all his money
8. talking monkey	8. lost his/her memory	8. joined the circus

9. overweight frog	9. caught a shark	9. got married
10. mad scientist	10. couldn't stop laughing	10. built a tepee
11. skinny football player	11. got lost in space	11. learned to read minds
12. canine detective	12. shrank to the size of an insect	12. learned to love everyone

After the three numbers have been selected—different combinations for each child—present each child with the story plots above, or replace characters, events, or results with those of your own choosing. Have each child find her predetermined parts of the story using the numbers selected. Review the different parts of a story and stress the need for elaboration and lots of colorful description to make the story as interesting as possible. (This can be accomplished by choosing a story plot orally with children or reading a model that you or other children have written.) Finally, have children write their stories using the predetermined plot, adding plenty of details as well as an original story ending (grades 3-6).

● **Imagine What Happens!** Select a picture story book that has much predictable dramatic intensity, such as *The King, the Cheese, and the Mice* or *The Gingerbread Rabbit*. Read the story aloud and stop at an exciting turning point in the story. Ask children to predict what might happen next using a "predictive web" on the blackboard or overhead, like so:

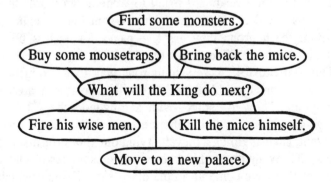

Then let children select one of the ideas brainstormed by the class, or another of their own, and write their version of the ending of the story. Allow children to then volunteer to read their original endings. Next read the real author's ending to the story to confirm or reject the children's hypotheses about what would happen. Emphasize that there is more than one way to end a story; the chances are that they have come up with some endings that are more interesting than the original author's! (Grades 3-6.)

• **Balloon Sensitivity.** Very beginning writers are often inspired most by concrete things that they can see, hear, and touch in the world around them. Help each child to blow up and tie a balloon. Next, divide children into groups of five. Give them a few moments to experiment with the balloon and their five senses: how does their balloon look, sound, smell, feel, and taste? Then give each child a sheet upon which is written one of the five sentence stems:

My balloon looks _____.
My balloon sounds _____.
My balloon smells _____.
My balloon feels _____.
My balloon tastes _____.

Explain that each child in a group will be responsible for **one** sensory statement about their balloon, e.g. "My balloon sounds squeaky" and will write their word on their page. The teacher should stand at the blackboard ready to write down words that need to be spelled. With individually-contributed balloon illustrations, each group now has five pages for a class book about balloons and the five senses (grades K-2).

• **How-To Stories.** A very humorous way to get reluctant writers to have an enjoyable experience with expository material is through the "how-to" story—with a tongue-in-cheek twist. Lead a general class discussion about certain skills that we need to be taught, such as riding a bicycle, tying our shoes, or making our beds, etc. Write on the blackboard some examples of "how to" phrases that have come up in the discussion. Explain which part is the infinitive (to tie) and which part is the direct object (our shoes). Next ask children to select their favorite "how to" phrase, write it on a small piece of paper, and then carefully tear it off between the infinitive and the direct object. Example:

How to milk   a cow

Then the teacher collects the direct objects and redistributes them to the children so that each child ends up with a rather comical combination phrase, e.g., "How to milk our shoes," that will no doubt inspire him to write a short, expository paragraph explaining in detail how to do this absurd task. Finally, make a class booklet, illustrated, to proudly share the products (grades 4-6).

   • **Story Starters.** Standard classroom fare for the reluctant writer is the "story starter" and many affective teachers regard this device as invaluable for getting children to begin writing. The most effective story starters are those that provide an exciting first sentence, a provocative accompanying illustration, and a list of four or five words that might be found in the story. Typed or neatly printed on 5"x8" cards, these "ignition keys" can be simply illustrated by the teacher or a student volunteer, or appropriate pictures can be cut from magazines and pasted onto the cards. Then the cards can be laminated, for durability, and placed in the classroom writing center to be used whenever a child needs some inspiration to start a story. Here are two examples of typical story starters (grades 2-6):

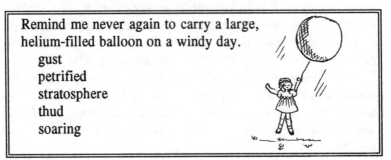

Remind me never again to carry a large, helium-filled balloon on a windy day.
   gust
   petrified
   stratosphere
   thud
   soaring

It was the smallest, most adorable pony
you have ever seen, and he had been
hiding under my bed.
   miniature
   whinny
   frightened
   secret
   shrunk

● **Mystery Boxes**. Bring in a large box upon which is painted in large block letters one or more of the following phrases: "Pandora's Box," "Spare Space Parts," "Captain Bluebeard's Treasure Chest," or "Danger! Do Not Open!" Allow the box to sit conspicuously in the room arousing the children's curiosity, but do not mention it directly or answer any questions about it. After a day or so, lead a general discussion about where such a box might have come from. Brainstorm some possible answers to these questions: Who might this box have belonged to? What might be in it? What do you feel certain is **not** in it? What are some things that might happen if we open it? Ask if any children have had similar experiences with mystery items that they have found. Finally, ask children to write a paragraph telling the story of the box—possible or impossible—and describing its supposed contents in detail. Note: Teachers have suggested two possible follow-ups to this activity: 1) the box is whisked away as mysteriously as it appeared; or 2) an encyclopedia is contained in the box, which is dramatically opened after the sharing of the stories. A discussion ensues about how knowledge can sometimes be "dangerous," but more often a "treasure" (grades 2-6).

● **Wishing on a Star**. With the children's input, write on the blackboard a number of things that can be wished upon, such as a wish bone, an eyelash, a penny thrown into a well, etc. Ask if anyone knows the poem about wishing on a star. Recite it together:

Star light, star bright,
First star I see tonight,
Wish I may, wish I might
Have the wish I wish tonight.

Encourage children to share some of the various things they have wished for. Then hand out lined ditto paper in the shape of a star and ask children to write about a time they remember when they wished upon a star (or an eyelash, or wish bone, etc.) and describe what happened after that. Did the wish come true? Did it cause the child to be happier or unhappier? Explain that their wish stories can be real or imaginary. Make a wishing bulletin board for those who want to share their products (grades 2-4).

• **What If...Stories.** Hypothetical situations are the kind of rich stimuli that turn the fantasizing of children into colorful stories. Every so often pose one of the following questions, or similar ones, to the class:

What would happen if you could have three wishes?
What if we could talk to animals?
What if you could read peoples' minds?
What if you could be invisible?
What if you could fly?
What if everyone looked exactly alike?
What if nobody ever got old?
What if you got younger, not older?
What if there is life on other planets?
What if you could always have everything you wanted?

When one of these "what if..." situations has been introduced, let each child take a few moments to think about how life would change for her. Then, with the use of the blackboard, have children contribute a list of possible advantages and disadvantages to the hypothetical situation actually occurring. Finally, ask each child to write down her version of what life would be like if this change actually were to happen (grades 2-6).

• **Scampering**. (Eberle, 1984). This innovative technique can help children understand how to generate new ideas by linking them with existing ones. It is useful as a prewriting strategy to be used in conjunction with any story from a basal reader or trade book. Following is an example of how the SCAMPERing acronym can be used to help children think about the story of *The Billy Goats Gruff* in fresh and original ways.

(S)**Substitute:** Ask children to consider what might have happened if the billy goats had had to go through a tunnel instead of across a bridge.

(C)**Combine:** Ask children to consider in which ways the three billy goats and the three little pigs are alike and different.

(A)**Adapt:** Ask children what they think might have happened if all three goats had tried to cross the bridge at the same time.

(M)**Modify:** Ask children what they think the troll might have done if the goats hadn't made any noise crossing the bridge.

(P)**Put to use:** In what other ways do children think the goats might have used their horns?

(P)**Point of view:** How do children think the story might be different if it were written from the point of view of the troll?

(E)**Eliminate:** Ask children to decide how the story would be changed if there were no troll.

(R)**Rearrange:** Ask children to imagine that the biggest goat had crossed the bridge first. How do children think the ending of the story would have been altered?

(R)**Reverse:** Ask children to rewrite the story as if the troll is trying to cross the goats' pasture, but they won't let him.

• **Cubing**. (Neeld, 1986). To help children organize their thoughts for essay writing, give them each a paper on which is drawn the sides for a cube, as in the following illustration. Instruct children to then write the following words, one on each side:

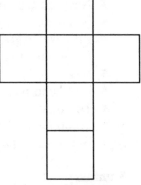

- Describe it
- Compare it (to something else)
- Associate it (with something else)
- Analyze it
- Apply it (to one's own life)
- Argue for it or against it

Then have children cut out the cube and assemble it. They are now able to hold in their hands a model that contains six ways to look at any topic, and a way to organize a six-paragraph essay. Offer the following possible topics and brainstorm some others:

friendship	city life
war	roller blading
pet ownership	gangs

Have the class select one of the above topics, or another of their own choosing. Divide the class into six cooperative groups. Assign each group one way to look at the topic (e. g., "describe it"). Encourage a recorder in each group to write down the group's ideas to be formed into a cohesive paragraph. Have a group leader from each group read the paragraphs aloud. Combine them into one six-paragraph essay.

- **Lists.** David Letterman's comedy routine of creating the "Ten Worst..." into a list provides a unique mode of discourse for children to explore. Categorizing skills are tapped, and the format used is simple enough for every learner. To initiate list writing, offer a topic such as "Ten Things that Make Me Mad." Then ask children to brainstorm some events that make them "mad" in small cooperative groups. Write on the chalkboard or overhead a couple of each group's responses to create a list of ten. Children are then ready to write their own individual lists. Provide some new ideas to motivate, but also invite children to brainstorm some suggestions.

Children can write the top ten things:
- Never to tell your mother.
- Never to tell a gorilla.
- I'll never regret.
- I don't understand.
- Never to do.
- I'd like to try.
- To do last.
- To do before breakfast.
- Not to ask a police officer.

Summary

Most affective teachers have a burning desire to open the flood gates of each and every one of their students so that each can experience the joy of self-expression through a satisfying creative outlet. When some children remain disinterested in writing and are continually moaning, "But I don't know what to write!" this can be a source of frustration to the conscientious teacher who wants to inspire **every** child to write. This chapter has offered teachers three different kinds of suggestions for dealing with the omnipresent reluctant writer: the first suggestion is for teachers to broaden their definition of what can be regarded as "creative" so that they might encourage the unique imaginative qualities that exist in every child. A more inclusive perspective of creativity will free children to experiment and take risks with language without fearing negative or restrictive evaluations.

The second set of suggestions deals with ways to create a classroom atmosphere most conducive to creative expression, where the gamut of ideas that children just naturally come up with can flourish and be recognized.

The final set of suggestions are specific writing activities that have been used successfully by practicing teachers to pique the imaginations of their reluctant writers. In an ideal affective language arts classroom these and other writing motivators are skillfully combined with an atmosphere that frees children to believe that they really can write because they have something exciting to say. That sad lament, "But I don't know what to write!" is gradually replaced with, "I can't write fast enough!" and it is indeed music to the affective teacher's ears.

References

Applegate, M. *Freeing Children to Write*. New York: Harper & Row, 1963.

Burton, W.H. and H. Hefferman. *The Step Beyond Creativity*. Washington DC: National Education Association of the United States, 1964.

Eberle, R. *Scamper On*. Buffalo, NY: D.O.K. Publishers, 1984.

Gurney, Nancy and Eric. *The King, the Mice and the Cheese*. New York: Random House, 1965.

Jarrell, R. *The Gingerbread Rabbit*. New York: Macmillan, 1964.

Chapter Six

Build-Me-Ups: Enhancing the
Self-Concept through the Language Arts

Jennifer is off to her first day at school. Will she be successful at learning how to read and write? Will she "pass" first grade? How can we predict?

More than likely, Jennifer has already been given an entire battery of tests to determine her state of readiness to begin reading and writing. She has been given intelligence tests, the verbal sections of which seem to be tied to later achievement in reading. She has also been given standardized reading readiness tests to see if her ability to make auditory and visual discriminations of letters and words is fine-tuned enough so that she will be as ready as others her age to learn to decode words. Additionally, Jennifer's teachers may have filled out check lists that help to show a profile of the child's mental alertness, her verbal prowess, and her ability to concentrate—all factors that help to signal that a child is ready to learn to read.

One crucial readiness area, however, is not routinely tested. It is an area that we know to be highly correlated with success in reading and writing; in fact, certain researchers go so far as to assert that it is THE most important predictor of success in reading: it is the "self-concept" of children like Jennifer and her classmates. We have indeed been aware since the early 1920s that a strong interactive effect exists between the self-concept and reading and writing success, yet we have failed to place a self-concept building program in most elementary curricula in any kind of thoughtful way, nor have we used it as a screening device for beginning reading instruction.

I remember countless curriculum planning meetings with classroom teachers and administrators to decide upon the educational goals for the coming academic year. Invariably, the enhancement of the self-concept of the children in the school would be mentioned as a global priority, and all the educators would solemnly avow that they were committed to the idea of improving the self-image of their charges. Yet these commitments always seemed to remain as lofty objectives, but were rarely translated into any real systematic classroom practice. What gives?

The reason for this apparent lack of carry-through may well be that there is no precise way to accurately measure the self-concept of children in numbers that will clearly go up, as achievement tests do, when we have made appropriate curriculum interventions. Particularly in our current climate of accountability for all that we do, pretests and post-tests are utilized to make most of the judgments about what is and what is not successful, with fractions of percentage points often dictating what will stay and what will be shelved in an academic program.

Although the self-concept cannot hope to be measured in such precise quantitative terms, the affective teacher, as a professional, should be the judge of whether the self-concept of each of her pupils is increasing or decreasing. She knows, because she is keenly tuned in to her pupils' feelings, but she may lack necessary statistics. She CAN show "numbers" in terms of the books that have been read, the number of pages written, the number of thoughts and ideas willingly shared, or the number of social overtures made by a once withdrawn child, but unfortunately, these are not the "magic figures" that carry clout in terms of accountability, even though they are desperately important.

An affective teacher need not lose heart, however. It is quite possible to add activities into the language arts program that have as their objectives the enhancement of the self-concept of children while giving them the kind of practice in reading, writing, listening, and speaking that will just naturally increase achievement scores in these areas. But like the other components in an affective language arts program, they will also help to create in children more positive attitudes toward themselves as readers, authors, and thinkers, as well as unique human beings.

Enhancing the Self-Concept of Second-Language Learners

Children for whom English is a second language have special needs, and for literacy to flourish, they must be in an environment that is particularly supportive and safe. Fitzgerald (1993) suggests that affective teachers can do several things to ensure a risk-taking environment in their classrooms, where ESL learners will have the best chance to grow in language skills while their self-concept is being enhanced. Teachers can:

• Model a love of language and frequently allow language play by inventing new words during reading and writing. Experiment with the sounds of language by reading playful books such as those written by Fred Gwynne and Dr. Seuss.

• Reward each and every attempt to read, write, listen, and speak. Praise ESL learners through gestures, praise, and positive facial expressions. Be encouraging of every effort ESL learners make at communicating and understanding.

• Don't worry about pronunciation and grammar mistakes in conversation, oral reading or writing. Respond to the meaning conveyed.

• Allow plenty of time for all language activities. Remember that learning a new language takes time!

• Talk to native English-speakers in the classroom about how they can help children who are at various stages of language development. Enlist their help in celebrating the successes of ESL learners and downplaying mistakes. Engage their curiosity about the culture and language of all diverse learners in the classroom.

Enhancing the Self-Concept through Bibliotherapy

An ideal way to develop the self-concept of children in an Affective Language Arts program is by showing them how to use literature to help them cope with their problems and identify with fictional characters who may have concerns similar to theirs. This process, called bibliotherapy, allows teachers to show children how certain books just naturally portray some of the conflicts that children may be facing in their lives. There are stories that can sensitize children to the plights of others who may be experiencing death, or divorce in their families, a physical or mental handicap, or perhaps just the "ordinary" pain that can come from the tribulations of being a child growing up in a most confusing world.

Bibliotherapy works when a bond begins to develop between the reader (or listener) and the main character in a story. A child typically goes through three stages toward greater self-understanding as a result of this bond: 1) identification, where the child feels close to the character because he begins to see that he is not the only one to have experienced this problem; 2) catharsis, when the child shares the characters' feelings as he works out the conflict in the story, and 3) insight, as the child's attitudes toward the problem are modified and the child feels a bit more confident about dealing with his problem (Corman, 1975).

To use bibliotherapy in an Affective Language Arts program, the teacher may on some occasions decide that the whole class needs to become more sensitive to a certain issue, such as racism. She would then select a book that deals with this theme, read it aloud to the class, and then discuss it with the class. In other cases, an individual child may be in much anguish when her mother remarries. In this instance, the teacher may suggest that that child read a book which deals sensitively with the problems that a stepchild may face. Later the teacher could ask the child how she felt about the main character and how she dealt with her problem. To assist a teacher in quickly identifying books that have the necessary themes at the appropriate age levels, *The Bookfinder* (Dreyer, 1977) is an invaluable resource. It contains over 1,100 children's books categorized into such topics as aggression, disabilities, death, divorce, moving and loneliness, and can help the teacher match a child who has a particular problem with a book that just might help him through it a little bit easier.

Another text of interest to teachers is *Developing Resiliency through Children's Literature*, (Cecil & Roberts, 1992) which identifies books with strong main characters who are able to cope with life's problems. The book summarizes over 200 titles and provides target activities that will help children learn to internalize the coping strategies used by the main characters.

The remainder of this chapter contains a panoply of other language arts activities designed to foster more positive self-concepts in children.

Activities to Create a Positive Classroom Climate

Welcoming Postcards. When the affective teacher first receives his class roster, a postcard can be sent to each of the new students explaining how very happy the teacher is to have this student in his class and describing a few highlights that the children can look forward to in the coming year.

Individual Chalkboards. When children are doing spelling, it is helpful for them to be able to write on individual chalkboards that can be made inexpensively out of cut pressed wood, masonite board, or similar substances and then painted over with chalkboard paint. Then, after spelling words have been dictated, the board can be held up for the teacher to correct. She can give each child a response without any of the other children seeing, so no child has to feel embarrassed in front of his peers.

Mail Service. A mailbox is a "must" in an affective classroom so that students can communicate in written form to each other and to the teacher. The teacher can utilize the service to reiterate that something in class was done particularly well or that the student has been especially kind to a troubled classmate, or any number of other messages that can make individual students feel better about themselves. The teacher can keep a roster of students' names to check off to make sure he is not overlooking any child.

Personalized Spelling. Using each child's name in spelling lists and spelling dictation is a wonderful way to combine enhancement of the self-concept with a basic spelling lesson. Students will learn how to spell each other's names and also discover new things about each other when the teacher dictates a sentence like, "Ramon likes to collect stamps of different countries."

Torture the Teacher. A great way to encourage students to gain positive academic self-images is to teach them some things that others (particularly adults!) do not know. This is especially true when working with children labeled "slow" or placed in special classes. In teaching spelling to such children, the teacher can include a few very difficult words, such as "proselytize" or "scrupulous," that even the so-called "smart" students don't know. Also, when starting a new unit in a content-area subject, the teacher can invite students to look through the text and find words that they think are unusually difficult to try to "stump" the teacher. If the teacher cannot correctly define the word or concept (and it is most helpful for affective teachers to admit that they do **not** know everything!), then the children "win."

Spread Rumors. Children feel very good about themselves when something they have done—a kind word or deed—has been recognized and affirmed. Teachers should make a point of describing such activities to the class without directly mentioning the student's name, but in a thinly-veiled manner. When a teacher says, "I noticed someone being especially courteous to Josh during recess," the entire class feels good.

Person of the Week. A bulletin board labeled "Very Important Person of the Week—(VIP)" can allow each child in your class to be highlighted and feel very special when he or she is featured. Baby pictures, toys that have been kept, plus a simple autobiography done by the parents with the child's help can be a self-concept enhancing focus of a classroom. The child can be encouraged during his week to tell the class about the baby pictures and read his autobiography or to tell a funny story about what he was told he did as a baby.

Activities to Create Confident Speakers and Writers

I Am. To highlight what makes individual children unique, children can draw a picture of themselves including any physical (or other) characteristic that makes them different from others. Then ask them to finish the sentence, "I am..." at least five times at the bottom of the drawing. Encourage them to elaborate on all the things that they feel contribute to making them unique. Provide some time when children can share their pictures and tell others a bit about themselves. Arrange the pictures around the room for several weeks to give all children a chance to look them over before they are taken down and put away for safekeeping to be used later in the year. This activity could be repeated toward the end of the year. If the class has spent much time in the interval in an Affective Language Arts program, obvious differences will be noted in the students' responses.

Be Your Thingo. A wonderful exercise that helps students explore the unique qualities of themselves and others in this class is "Be Your Thingo." Each child is given a dittoed grid portioned off like a bingo card. Then a master card with instructions is put on the blackboard or overhead so that students know what to write in each space. Next, students are asked to write in the appropriate words and phrases to describe their characteristics. Then the students write each of these characteristics on a small square of paper so that it can be put in the "pot." Beans are used as markers and the game then proceeds like bingo. Example:

— THINGO —

Colors	Name	Place	Family Members	Likes
your hair (brown)	yours (Ben)	born (Indiana)	me (brother)	1st choice (camping)
your eyes (brown)	mother (Heather)	would like to go (Australia)	mother 	2nd choice (reading)
your house (red)	a friend (Ray)	wouldn't like to go (South Africa)	father	3rd choice (football)
favorite (light blue)	favorite (Matt)	have visited (Canada)	brother or sister (Rian)	4th choice (baseball)
least favorite (light green)	book character (Sherlock)	have read about (Israel)	pet (fish)	doesn't like (jump rope)

I'm For Sale! After a unit on newspapers or advertising techniques, a good way to incorporate enhancement of the self-concept is by asking students to write original advertisements trying to "sell" themselves. First, the students must think about their best qualities as well as several things that they are able to do well. Then these positive items are integrated into the ad along with some salient "likes" and "dislikes." For example,

"For Sale: A tennis-playing eleven-year-old girl with freckles, pig-tails (sometimes) and a sunny disposition. Very friendly and likes to talk to everyone. Likes her room very neat, but doesn't like spinach. Is able to sew and knit wonderful things, but is also in Little League. Reasonable."

Picture Perfect. To encourage each child in the class to begin to focus on the positive, rather than the negative qualities of each other, take photographs of each child and hang them up around the room. Discuss with the class that every person has good qualities and the class will be exploring these for each member of the class. Any time they wish to, they may write something "true" and "good" about a person in the class under his or her picture. The teacher, too, should feel free to add comments and encourage the children to read and discuss the comments written on the sheets of other classmates. At the end of the week, have a discussion about how people's attitudes change toward each other when they are concentrating on and looking for only the good.

Person Match. To help children develop relationships based upon respect and understanding, and to bring out the "shy" child, have students complete these sentence starters on a 3"x5" card, such as:

My favorite song is_____.
The place I go to be alone is_____.
The person I most admire is_____.
If I could have one wish, I'd wish for_____.
The best book I ever read was_____.

Instruct students **not** to put their names on their papers, and distribute them, making sure no child gets his or her own. After all students have read the answers, children try to find the person who wrote the paper by asking questions based upon the information given in the paper, e.g., "Is Mother Teresa the person you admire most?" Even if the answer is "no," the person must share who the person he admires most is. Students sit down and chat with their person when they have found him.

Lifelines. In order to fully appreciate why they are the way they are, children must learn to reflect on the important events of their lives. A good precursor to an autobiography is to ask students to list the five most important things that have happened in their lives and to write down how old they were when these events occurred. Then help them to make a scroll using parchment paper attached to two popsicle sticks. Help them to place their events in the order in which they took place (most children begin with their birth). Let them make a brief presentation to the class about their choices. They then have an outline to fill in for their autobiographies.

Activities to Create Children Confident In Oral Language

Who Are You? To help children to identify what is unique and special about themselves, a series of forced-choice questions can be asked that allow them to creatively reflect upon their personal qualities. Children are asked, Are you more like...
   ...a rose or a dandelion? Why?
   ...the sun or the moon? Why?
   ...cotton or wool? Why?
   ...a cat or a dog? Why?
   ...red or blue? Why?
   ..."head in the clouds" or "feet on the ground"? Why?
   ...breakfast or lunch? Why?
   ...the mountains or the ocean? Why?
   ...fall or spring? Why?
   ...a baby or an elderly person? Why?
After children have written down their responses, ask for volunteers to tell orally why they chose the answers they did. Emphasize that there are many different ways to be, which is why the world is such an interesting place!

Happy Circle. A routine that goes a long way toward encouraging children to look at the positive things in themselves and others and helps them to feel comfortable sharing in front of a group is the happy circle. For a few minutes every day, children sit in a circle and everyone gets to add one thought to a common theme, such as saying one positive thing about a selected student, e.g., "I like the way Wendy smiles," or "Wendy is always there with a joke; she makes me happy when I feel bad." Or the circle might begin with everyone relating one positive thing that has happened that day, or "one thing that made me happy today." Done on a daily basis, this technique goes a long way toward building healthy self-images and improved interpersonal relationships, as well as confident speakers.

Slogan Statements. What people say through their T-shirts and on their bumper stickers can tell us something about their beliefs. Over a two or three day period children can keep a list of the slogans that they notice on people's T-shirts and bumper stickers. Collect the lists. Have children play a combination of twenty questions and charades by first having other classmates figure out the slogans by using only questions that can be answered "yes" or "no." Then, if it is unlikely the slogan has been heard before, charades can be used to get the specific words. As slogans are guessed, write them on the blackboard. Afterwards, have a discussion about why people might advertise their beliefs in this manner and what can be learned about them from the slogans they display.

The Secret Me. For several days, have children collect things from home and at school to go on a collage—things they like to do, places they have been, people they admire, possessions, opinions, etc. Display anonymous collages around the room. Beneath each one put a box. Children can then try to guess who each collage belongs to and why, and put that child's name in the box. Then let each child share his or her collage and the meaning of the items in it. Discuss what surprises cropped up. Then talk about the damage that can be done when opinions based on preconceptions of a person are made before actually getting to know that person.

Good and Bad. This activity shows children how it feels to receive negative or preferential treatment based upon superficial characteristics. After allowing two or three students to leave the room, choose a characteristic such as the opposites "short" and "tall." Then go around the room telling tall students they are "bad" and short ones they are "good." The children who left the room then return and try to guess the criterion by which the students were labeled. After several rounds, explore such concepts as value judgments, stereotyping and prejudicial treatment. Solicit input from those who were labeled to see how they felt when others were responding to them negatively. What were their feelings toward those placing arbitrary value judgments upon them? Then contrast the feelings of the "good" and "bad" students. A lot of insights can occur.

Natural Resources. Often children feel powerless when they can indeed do many things, but haven't considered all the things they can do. Their self-worth can be enhanced by asking them to make a list of all the things they can do such as sew, paint, rake leaves, read, dance, tell jokes, do dishes, etc. Then they can be instructed to consider what tools they have at their disposal to accomplish some of the things they can do. These items might be things like a rake, needle and thread, cooking utensils, etc. Then, have them draw an outline of themselves and on the picture they can write, "I can do these things; I can use these tools." Have them cut out their outlines and paste them on a piece of construction paper and decorate it to look like themselves. Hang these from the ceiling over each child's desk. For several days emphasize the idea that "we have a roomful of marvelous human resources and potential" and let them discuss their abilities.

Acrostic Poems. Children feel good about themselves when their special qualities are recognized by others. The acrostic poem lets them concentrate on each other's positive qualities. After dividing children into pairs, let each write a simple, unrhymed poem about the other child using the letters in the other child's name to start each phrase. All phrases must reflect some "good" and "true" qualities in the other child. Example:

Never a frown,
Always smiling,
Not a care in the world,
Can you be her friend?
You will want to be!

Let the writer of the poem read it while the recipient of such positive comments beams!

Who Are You? Interviewing skills can be enhanced while children learn to better appreciate one another through this activity: After pairing off students (the more unlikely the pair, the better!), tell them they are going to make a book about the person with whom they are paired. Each week allow the pairs to meet for twenty minutes to discuss past events ("When did you learn to walk and talk?") or recent events in the lives of their partners ("What did you do over summer vacation?"). Then let the children write about what was discussed in the current session, illustrating the piece if desired. At the end of the school year, each child will have a biography presented to him or her that can be shared with the class and read again and again.

Summary

Although educators have known for years that the self-concept is strongly related to successful achievement in all facets of language skills, most schools have not placed the enhancement of the self-concept into their curriculum in any systematic way. This may be because teachers and administrators are keenly aware of the need for achievement scores that reflect growth in academic areas, and the improvement of the self-concept is not easily put into numbers, even though the majority of practitioners include it among their primary goals for their students. Fortunately, there are ways to enhance the self-concept of children through activities that also give much-needed practice in the language arts of reading, writing, speaking, and listening.

Bibliotherapy is a technique that can be used in an Affective Language Arts program to aid children in their ability to come to terms with their problems and to feel more capable of their ability to handle them. The affective teacher can help match a child to a main character with a similar concern through the use of *The Bookfinder* which contains over 1,100 titles categorized by subject area and age level.

To enhance the self-concept of her children, the affective teacher need not sacrifice sound teaching that will help her students to achieve in the language arts. Fortunately, there are many classroom activities that skillfully combine the language arts of reading, writing, speaking, and listening with the enhancement of the self-concept by having children discover new things about each other and teaching them to look for the positive qualities in each other as well as themselves. Many such activities have been described in this chapter.

References

Beane, J. and R.R. Lipka. *Self-Concept, Self-Esteem and the Curriculum*. Boston: Allyn and Bacon, 1984.

Cecil, N.L. and P.L. Roberts, *Developing Resiliency Through Children's Literature: A Guide for Teachers and Librarians, K-8*. Jefferson, NC: McFarland, 1992.

Corman, C. "Bibliotherapy—Insight for the Learning Handi-capped." *Language Arts* 52, No. 8 (1975): pp. 935-37.

Dreyer, S.S. *The Bookfinder*. Circle Pines, MN: American Guidance Service, 1985.

Edwards, P.A. and L. Simmons. "Bibliotherapy: A Strategy for Communication Between Parents and their Children." *Journal of Reading* 30, No. 2 (1986): pp. 819-21.

Fitzgerald, J. "Literacy and Students Who are Learning English as a Second Language." *The Reading Teacher* 46, No. 8, (May) 1993: pp. 638-647.

Gibson, J.T. *Psychology for the Classroom*. Englewood Cliffs, NJ: Prentice-Hall, 1976.

Hummel, J. and N.L. Cecil. "Self-Concept and Academic Achievement." *Journal of Humanistic Education and Development* 42, No. 1, 1984: pp. 12-21.

Purkey, W. *Self-Concept and School Achievement*. Englewood Cliffs, NJ: Prentice-Hall, 1970.

Siccone, F. and J. Canfield. *101 Ways to Develop Student Self-Esteem and Responsibility*, Vol. 1. Boston: Allyn and Bacon, 1993.

Chapter Seven

The Newspaper: Conduit to Our Reading Culture

While visiting small fishing villages along the Eastern seaboard of Canada, I have been continually fascinated by the ease with which children living in these tiny villages become active members of their fishing culture. From the time they can first walk and talk they joyfully experience all the facets of fishing, from making the fishing nets to the intricacies of baiting and casting a line. To such children these activities are as natural as breathing. Because their parents and everyone they know participate in some aspect of fishing, the children, too, grow up learning to fish and enjoy it.

Thus it should be in our culture with reading. The activity is certainly as necessary for survival in our society, yet reading is not an activity that is visibly modeled by all adults in our culture. So unfortunately, the message that reading is a vital activity does not naturally come across to our children as strongly and loudly as we might hope.

One type of reading, however, seems to be more visibly modeled than others by adults in our culture; indeed, it might be considered to be as much a part of the American lifestyle as the morning cup of coffee: the local newspaper, though not often lauded for its literary merit, belongs in an Affective Language Arts program because it is one of THE major reading activities by which we demonstrate that we really are a reading culture. For children to become familiar with this pervasive adult institution is to have them begin to take part in a tradition that they are apt to see many adults modeling on a routine basis.

Another reason for including the newspaper in an Affective Language Arts program is that children get to see another valid reason for reading—to gain information about what is currently

91

happening in the world. Unfortunately, the major thrust in many language arts programs is often so heavily geared toward story or narrative structure—picture story books in the primary grades evolving to short novels in the intermediate grades—that we tend to overlook the fact that for some children (and adults) reading for information will always be the preferred genre. We have for too long subtly implied to children that only those who love reading "books" and "novels" could possibly be considered true lovers of reading! This is as sad as it is untrue.

For these reasons, I have chosen to include a chapter which looks at how the local newspaper can be used in an Affective Language Arts program. This chapter will include activities to familiarize children with the newspaper, and activities that stimulate them to write and think critically, as well as a section on creating a classroom newspaper. Additionally, "just for fun" newspaper activities are included for the purpose of building positive associations with this important conduit to our reading culture.

Introducing Children to the Newspaper

Perhaps the best way to introduce children to the newspaper is to initially discuss some of the vocabulary that is common to this particular medium: editorial, obituary, headline, dateline, advice column, classified, advertisement, horoscope, weather, entertainment, index, and features, are a few of the words and phrases with which they need to become familiar. Besides using these words as the weekly spelling lesson, a scavenger hunt can be employed to make sure that children can find examples of each of these items by looking carefully through the newspaper.

A subsequent scavenger hunt might require children to scout through the newspaper to find these items that can be found daily in every newspaper:

A picture of an animal	A comic strip
A famous sports figure	A fact
A word describing you	A graph or chart
A crime committed	Name of your state

A crossword puzzle   Another word game
An ad for a car   An opinion
A movie you want to see   A TV show you like
A crisis situation

To show children the scope of services provided by the newspaper, have them participate in a third scavenger hunt that instructs them to look for specific advertisements that might appeal to the following groups:

Men   Mothers
Women   All adults
People looking for   People wanting to save
  recreation   money
People needing a   People looking for
  vacation   a new home
Children   People with pets
People who smoke   People with a hobby
People in search of a job   People who are hungry

To graphically illustrate to children the way headlines are used to grab people's attention with a minimum of words, the teacher can write the headline, "Teacher Caught Stealing" on the blackboard. Solicit many ideas as to what this headline might mean. Then explain that this headline is the lead-in for an article about a local faculty-student softball game in which the music teacher was tagged while attempting to "steal" second base! Let children draw their own conclusions as to why such a deliberately misleading headline might have been created for the article. Then encourage children to try to find other headlines that attract attention in a similar way.

Finally, to help children to begin to understand the succinct nature of newspaper journalism, have them practice choosing articles and then determining just how quickly the facts of "who," "what," "when," "where," "why," and "how" are revealed. After doing some practice articles orally with the whole class, let children pair off, select an article, and then answer these questions which can be typed onto a ditto master:

What is the headline of your article?
Who is the subject(s) of your article?
What is the main idea, or topic, of your article?
When did the event take place?
Where did the event take place?
According to your article, **why** did the event take place?
How is the event happening?

Using the Newspaper to Motivate Writing

After children have become familiar with the newspaper and feel comfortable working with it, the following activities can be used to stimulate writing.

● **Antonyms.** Have children look through advertisements in the paper to find a product that they dislike. Have them make a list of positive descriptions that have been used and then find words that mean just the opposite of these words. Instruct them to then rewrite the advertisement telling people what the product is **really** like, in their opinion.

● **Questions.** Help children to select a feature article which interests them, such as a piece about a recent lottery winner. Ask them to write a list of ten questions they would like to ask the person if they had the opportunity to interview him or her. Then have them make some predictions about what possible responses might be based upon their hunches about the individual.

● **Imaginary Conversations.** Students will enjoy finding pictures of two people in the news with whom they are especially fascinated. Instruct them to place the two pictures on top of a piece of paper to look as though the two people are having a conversation. Using dialogue format, have children then make up the fictional conversation that might have taken place between the two individuals—in a humorous or serious vein.

● **Lost and Found.** From the classified ads in the newspaper have children select an item that has been either lost or found and then let them write a short piece—silly or serious—about how that item came to be lost or found, who lost it, where it was lost, and the feelings of the person who lost (or found) it.

- **Recipes**. Encourage children to find a recipe in the newspaper that sounds like a food they might enjoy eating. Point out how the ingredients are usually listed in a recipe, but that often the directions for combining the items are not clearly sequenced for the reader. Ask the children to rewrite the instructions in a paragraph format, using words that clearly signify sequence, such as "first," "next," "then," "finally," etc. Then let them actually prepare their chosen food and write a critique of the results in the same language that the restaurant critic in the newspaper might use.

- **Mock Mugging**. Help a group of students to prepare to stage a "mock mugging" or accident for the rest of the class. Instruct other members of the class to write a newspaper article about the incident as they saw it. Encourage class members to formulate questions for interviews with the "victims" and other persons involved in the mock incident. Discuss variations in the written accounts of the incident and brainstorm some possible reasons for the variations as well as the implications of those variations for the readers of the news.

- **Controversy**. Guide a class discussion about some controversial topic of current interest in the news, such as the efficacy of nuclear power. In two separate columns on the blackboard or overhead, write down children's comments, pro and con, about the issue. Then encourage each child to write an editorial (his or her personal opinion) on the topic.

- **Personal Letters**. Have students find a feature article about someone who has experienced a major good or bad event recently—for example, the loss of a beloved animal, winning the lottery, or some personal triumph over adversity. Review the different reasons one might have for writing a letter to someone—to express sympathy, to extend congratulations, etc. Let children draft a letter to the person they have selected from the newspaper. After revising and editing letters with the help of peer editors and/or a teacher conference, let the children send their letters to their chosen person, in care of the local newspaper.

● **Restaurant Critic.** After discussing the specific style of writing of restaurant critics, allow children to review (tactfully) a lunch served in the school cafeteria, or a bag lunch from home. If the class has its own newspaper, encourage children to let the review become a standard feature of the paper.

● **Smart Consumer.** Have children find a half page or full page advertisement in the newspaper. Tell them to read all the information in the ad and then write down all the factual information that is included about the product, deliberately ignoring any glamorous or "hype" words. Based upon this activity, have them then write a paragraph stating whether or not they would buy the product and why or why not. Encourage them to also include any additional information they might need before they could make a decision.

Activities to Expand Critical Thinking

Newspapers can provide some excellent fodder for critical thinking, and provide a more realistic context and refreshing change from workbooks purporting to teach these skills. With teacher guidance, children can grow in their ability to analyze information through the following activities:

● **Analyzing an Article.** Have the children find an article in the paper that relates to a topic that they have been studying. Then ask them to complete these steps for analyzing the article: 1) Read the article carefully; 2) Circle the important facts and factual statements; 3) Write a summary of the article; 4) Identify the topic that they have already studied and explain how the article relates to it; 5) List any new information that has been gained about the topic.

● **Facts and Opinions.** From the editorial page, let children choose an editorial. Divide the blackboard or overhead into two sections, labeled "Facts" and "Opinions." On the fact side, solicit from the children all the statements that can be proven. On the opinion side write down all statements that are just one person's opinion. Help children to look for techniques that might lead them to question what the author is saying: Does the author show bias? Are the author's ideas based on faulty assumptions? Does the author use any propaganda techniques (e.g. emotionally laden words or name-calling)?

- **Article Summaries**. After students have selected an article of their choice, have them read it carefully and respond to the following questions:

1) What are two conclusions you could draw from your article?

2) What are some questions you would like to ask the writer of this article?

3) What are some ways the information in this article could affect you?

4) What groups of people might be pleased by the information in this article?

5) What groups of people might be upset by the information in this article?

- **Time Capsule**. Tell students to imagine that they are in charge of preparing a time capsule for children in the year 3000. They would want to reveal to the people of that era as much as they could about life today. Instruct them to cut out the ten items (using pictures or words) from the newspaper that would best describe what their life is like. Allow children to orally defend their selections.

- **SQ3R**. Newspapers provide excellent practice material for study skills. Have each child choose an article. Then ask each child to go through the following five steps:

1) Skim your article quickly.

2) List four questions you have about your article.

3) Read your article to answer your questions.

4) Rewrite the article, answering your own questions.

5) Recite from memory all you have learned from the article.

6) List any questions you still have about the topic.

- **Political Propaganda**. Instruct children to find examples of candidates' campaign statements. Divide the blackboard or overhead into two columns: specific and general. Solicit responses from children about each statement as to whether it gives very general promises or solutions to problems, or very specific, explicit ideas as to what the candidate will really do.

● **Community Concerns.** Let children select articles from the local newspaper about city problems such as water shortages, traffic congestion, vandalism, etc., and have them make suggestions as to how each problem might be solved. After brainstorming as a class, encourage children to write letters to appropriate city officials outlining their recommendations for solutions.

Just For Fun

The following motivational activities tend to promote growth in the various subskills of the language arts and are valuable with all grade levels to help build positive associations with the newspaper:

● **Cartoon Dialogue.** From the comics section, have each child cut out a favorite cartoon. Let each paste his cartoon on construction paper and then use white-out to erase the dialogue in the cartoon bubble. Instruct each child to look at the cartoon and, from the action portrayed by the pictures, write new dialogue in his own words.

● **How-To.** Ask children to find a "how-to" article from the home section of the newspaper. Show them how to write each step on a separate strip of paper. Mix the steps and allow children to exchange their how-to articles and attempt to put them back into the correct sequence.

● **Sports Verbs.** Discuss with children several examples of terms used on the sports page to denote that one team has triumphed over the other: "Cubs **blitz** the Red Sox"; "Lakers **jolt** Kings." Keep a running classroom list of all the different verbs that are used to indicate success and failure in the sports headlines.

● **Match the Headlines.** Cut out articles from the newspaper and paste them on construction paper or tagboard. Separate the headlines from the articles and place several combinations in a bag. Ask children to shake the bag, select an article, skim it, and then see if they can find the appropriate headline for that article.

• **My S-E-L-F.** Have children cut out the capital letters that make up their first names from the headlines in the newspaper. Then ask them to look through the rest of the paper for twenty-five words that they feel describe who they are. Help them to paste the words, collage-fashion, on sheets of colored construction paper.

• **Mars Adventure.** Tell children they are about to go on a pretend adventure to the planet Mars for an extended period of time. Instruct them to look through the newspaper, find, and cut out five items (using only pictures or words) that they feel would best help them survive their ordeal. Advise them that their allotted space would be no larger than their desks. Have them paste their five items on construction paper and then orally defend their choices.

• **Newsmakers.** Make a bulletin board of photos of people who are currently in the news. Put a blank sheet of paper underneath each person and allow children to cut out and paste words from the newspaper which describe each person.

• **Mystery Person.** From the newspaper have each child cut out appropriate words and phrases to fill in the following blanks:

My age is _____.
My favorite food is _____.
My favorite sport is _____.
I sometimes wear _____.
I can be described as _____.
My favorite TV show is _____.
This makes me angry: _____.
This makes me happy: _____.

Collect the "mystery" sheets and read them out loud. Let children try to guess who each mystery person is.

• **Rapid Recall.** Ask each child to choose an interesting picture from the newspaper. Allow each child to study her picture carefully for two minutes. Then tell all the children to turn their pictures over and try to write down as many things as they can remember about their picture. Then let pairs of children evaluate each other's recall.

● **Role Plays**. From an advice column such as Dear Abby have several children role play a situation of their choosing. Let other children in the class volunteer to get up and simulate possible solutions to the problem. Discuss the benefits of each suggested solution.

Creating a Classroom Newspaper

After children have become familiar with the newspaper and its particular brand of journalism, they will often be eager to institute their own classroom newspaper. This venture is an optimal way to provide plenty of integrated reading, writing and re-writing practice. Additionally, it serves as an important forum for the publication of children's work, and reinforces content area curricular classroom activities and field trips by allowing children to write about them for their own paper.

I can best attest to the value of a classroom newspaper from my own experience: I don't remember the publication of my first journal article as a professor nearly as vividly as I do the time I had an article published in our sixth-grade newspaper. The positive feedback I was given from teachers and peers is still fresh in my memory. Many children have told me similar tales of their feelings about having published their work in classroom newspapers.

Having children select a name for the classroom newspaper is crucial because it clearly establishes the students' ownership and authorship of the project. Allow children to first do some research into some names of local newspapers and then encourage the whole class to vote on a name that is personal yet in the language of newspapers—such as "The Sixth Grade Centurion" or "The Renton School Reporter."

Next it is time to decide how the class newspaper will be produced. Help the children discuss the following issues:

1) Will the newspaper be photocopied or mimeographed?
2) Will you sell the papers for a fee, or will the class ask for help from the PTA?
3) Will the paper be sold to the whole school, or just the class that is producing the paper?
4) Do you want to include art work?
5) Will the newspaper be typed or printed?
6) Who will duplicate the paper?

Organizing the Class

Let the class determine an editor for each page. That editor will be responsible for all the stories and art work on that page. The teacher can serve as "publisher" and thus supervise all work, but the class should agree on and set deadlines and the publication date.

As a class, discuss the stories that must be in the paper and the stories that would be desirable. The class newspaper should contain news stories, feature stories, sports and editorials. To keep the newspaper current, have children check the school calendar and plan which events to cover and promote in the paper. The following are other possibilities to consider as part of the paper:

Book review	Classified
Advice column	Advertisements
Weather report	Crossword puzzle
School lunch review	School-wide contests
Fun page-jokes, riddles	Original stories and poems

Each editor should make an assignment sheet for his page and post it where everyone can see it. The editor may assign stories to certain students in the class, or children may sign up for the stories they wish to write. In either case, the teacher and editors should see that every child, including the editors, makes at least one written contribution.

Features, Sports and Editorial

Feature stories can allow children to interview people involved in significant school events and create human interest, instead of the usual news story written in the past tense. Feature writers should be encouraged to write stories that are more creative and less "condensed" than news stories.

Sports writers should know that their best choice for the classroom newspaper would be the sports feature story, allowing them to do in-depth interviews with a team member or a story about the sport itself.

Caution students about editorials: guide them to realize, through their familiarity with "real" editorials, that this piece of writing can commend as well as criticize something. Tell children that an editorial should state a problem, analyze it, and then offer a constructive solution. Stress that any editorials printed must be fair, and provide space for letters to the editors by readers who disagree with the editor's point of view.

Editing and Layout

When the stories are finished, they should first be read by the editor, then revised and resubmitted if the editor suggests any changes. If there are none, the child should schedule a conference with the teacher to go over the story for any mechanical problems. When the story has been rewritten to the satisfaction of the student, the editor, and the teacher, it should be put in an envelope for the page on which it is supposed to appear. The editor should then check off each completed story on the assignment sheet.

Once all the stories for a page are finished, the editor should take a sheet of paper the size of the completed newspaper page and lay out the page, noting where each story and piece of artwork is to be placed.

The most important story on each page should be placed in the upper left-hand corner, except for the front page, where it should be placed in the upper right-hand corner.

Each story should have a headline, which will typically grab the reader's attention with a minimum of words. Headlines can be typed or hand lettered on the master.

The art work needs to be measured exactly for size and space left for it on the master so that it can be transferred just before the paper is mimeographed or photocopied.

Then the stories, headlines, and art work should be sent to the typist, word processor or hand printer. When the papers come back, they should be proofread and corrected by the editors and teacher before being run off.

When the pages have been run off, they can be collated and stapled by the class. Distribution might take place at lunchtime, before or after school, or to individual classrooms. A treasurer should be appointed to keep track of all money received.

Summary

Newspapers can be dynamic teaching tools for an Affective Language Arts program. The wide scope of material in the average local newspaper makes it an ideal stimulus for critical thinking and a wide array of writing activities that cross the entire curriculum. Additionally, many of the subskills of the language arts can be practiced and reinforced in motivational ways using some of the newspaper exercises suggested in this chapter. Too, familiarity with the newspaper's format and style of journalism often spurs children to want to develop their **own** classroom newspaper, providing an excellent forum for the students' own writing. Thus, an even more pressing reason to complete the arduous task of writing, revising, and editing naturally comes to light in the classroom.

Perhaps more importantly, though, children start to recognize the value of newspapers in a free and literate society. They begin to take part in one of the few reading activities in American culture that is actively modeled and enjoyed by a large number of adults on a routine basis. When they have been introduced to the "newspaper habit," children feel they have somehow entered the grown-up world of our reading culture. Though some children may never grow up and experience the joys of the wide spectrum of other literary genres available to them, at least this one important door will have been opened wide.

Chapter Eight

The Wonder of Words

Since words are the obvious building blocks of sentences and thus ALL writing, a classroom in which the teacher and children enjoy playing with words is usually one in which children also enjoy writing. In such a classroom, all the children are delighted when Chrissy suddenly chirps, "A clink is like a pink drink of water!" because word play is just naturally pleasing to their ears, and they know the teacher thinks so too. In such a classroom, also, when John asks how to spell the word "succeed" because he wants it for his journal entry, the teacher does not demand that he "look it up." The wise teacher realizes that this would be one of the surest ways to dampen John's burgeoning enthusiasm for the dictionary as the "house of words," and she is also quite certain that the next time he would hesitate before asking for her assistance when spelling a word he didn't know. So, instead, she patiently shows him how to spell his word so that he can get back, without serious interruption, to the important business of writing down his thoughts.

Because children begin their lives with an intense curiosity about words, the affective teacher of language arts has a very special mission in regard to the teaching of vocabulary. She can: 1) perpetuate the children's interest (if she is lucky, and too many "look it ups" haven't already destroyed it); or she can 2) try to rekindle the interest if she finds that her students have become dictionary-shy and word-weary; or, 3) she can actively build into her language arts program some exciting activities that can help make vocabulary development an outgrowth of children's natural linguistic play, rather than the more common tedium of looking up isolated words and then writing them in sentences that occurs in drearier classrooms.

This chapter contains suggestions to make the third option a reality. A potpourri of teacher-tested activities will be described that can be used to cultivate, nourish, and enrich children's listening, speaking, reading, and writing vocabularies. Activities are also included for the purpose of building positive associations with the dictionary as a useful "friend" that tells readers and writers things they want to know about words. Finally, a few words of caution are offered about some unfortunate prevalent practices that can easily extinguish the love of learning flame. Instead, by implementing some of the ideas set forth in this chapter, teachers can actively fan the flame by encouraging children's natural fascination with words. Such teachers will more than likely be rewarded with students who will risk penning their ideas in fresh and interesting ways.

Stimulating Interest in Words

Teachers can help children appreciate the connection between words in our language through an enjoyable look at some verbal relationships via these vocabulary-enriching activities.

• **Novel Appellations.** Children are intrigued by adages such as the following examples for which synonyms have been used for each original word or phrase, although the meaning has been kept intact. Introduce children to the Thesaurus as an invaluable aid in translating them:

Members of an avian species of identical plumage congregate. (Birds of a feather flock together.)

All articles that coruscate with resplendence are not necessarily auriferous. (All that glitters is not gold.)

The stylus is more potent than the claymore. (The pen is mightier than the sword.)

Male cadavers are incapable of yielding testimony. (Dead men tell no tales.)

It is fruitless to attempt to indoctrinate a superannuated canine with innovative maneuvers. (You can't teach an old dog new tricks.)

After "decoding" these sentences into their more common form, children will be eager to similarly encode other common phrases, titles of books, or popular songs with the help of the Thesaurus, for other members of the class to decode. A further challenge is to ask them to design phrases that mean the opposite of the originals that they have collected. For example, "All that glitters is not gold," might become, "None that tarnishes is silver."

● **Classifying Grid.** To allow children to gain enjoyable practice categorizing words, a classifying grid can be used. The name of a child in the class is selected and then other class members determine five to ten categories that they would like to encounter. Then in groups of four or five, children try to fill in the grid, trying to think of an item to fill every cell, as in the following grid:

	J	**A**	**N**	**E**
animal	jaguar	armadillo	newt	elephant
tree	juniper	ash	nut	elm
flower	jonquil	azalea	narcissus	Easter lily
food	jam	asparagus	nutbread	egg
color	jade	avocado	nilegreen	eggshell
country	Japan	Antarctica	Nigeria	Ethiopia

To score the grid, groups get one point for every cell that is correctly filled in and three points for items that no other group mentioned.

   • **Semantic Mapping.** An excellent way to help children understand how words relate to one another is through the semantic map. This technique can span all content areas and is especially useful for crystallizing concepts with which students have been introduced. Before or after studying gas, for example, children can be asked to contribute everything they can think of about the subject while the teacher records what is said in columns on the blackboard, according to the categories in which they might fit. With the teacher's guidance, the children later go back and label the categories, gaining a much greater insight into how the more abstract, superordinate concepts, and the concrete, subordinate concepts might fit together, like so:

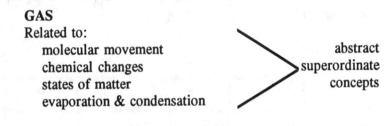

GAS
Related to:
    molecular movement
    chemical changes
    states of matter
    evaporation & condensation

    abstract
superordinate
    concepts

Uses	**Kinds**	**Properties**
heating	natural	expands
illuminating	helium	colorless
putting people	neon	fills space
to sleep	chlorine	no volume

more concrete
subordinate
concepts

Understanding the major meaning-bearing affixes in our language can be extremely helpful when trying to determine the meaning of unfamiliar words, but can also become a creative and motivational classroom project by implementing this teacher-tested idea:

   • **Wacky Word Book.** After some direct instruction about the organization of a dictionary and the meaning of some of our most commonly used roots, prefixes, and suffixes, children will be interested in creating their own classroom dictionary of "wacky words." The teacher can give each child a list of these roots and affixes and then group children into threes to cooperatively create a list of ten "new" words by combining prefixes, suffixes, and roots in novel ways. Next the groups should be instructed to think up some humorous (or realistic) meanings for their newly coined words. Examples:

au'to.therm"ist, n. one who sets himself on fire.

cir'cum-hy.dri"tis, n. the state of walking around puddles instead of through them.

mul'ti.vi"tish, adj. having several lives.

ret'ro.cel"er.ide, n. the act of running quickly backwards.

Then each group should present its new words to the other members of the class who can try to guess the definitions of the words from their own knowledge of the various word parts. Finally, the class can create their own "wacky word book" for publication by entering all their new entries into a dictionary.

An understanding of how words can be used to actually "paint pictures," much as an artist mixes colors to get just the right hues, can be developed by helping children to become aware of the fine shades of meanings of words in our language. The next two activities can help to heighten this awareness:

• **Cloze Stories.** To use the instructional cloze to build an appreciation of fine shades of meaning, the teacher can take a short (approximately 250 words) article from a children's magazine, a young people's encyclopedia, or even a lengthy advertisement from the newspaper, and delete every other adjective. She should then display the original passage, with deletions, on an overhead projector, after children have filled in their own adjectives. Let the children then contribute their own word choices for the deletions. Discuss with children how certain words make a clearer visual picture for the reader than others. For example, in the sentence, "The _____ lady lumbered down the street," the use of the word "lumbered" should suggest to children that the lady talked about is quite large, and a choice of the word "obese," "hefty," or "stout" for the blank would make the image more clear than the choice of a more generic word such as "big." Stress that while many words are acceptable, there are some words that serve to enlighten the reader more completely than others.

● **Assembling and Disassembling Sentences.** An excellent way to teach subject and predicate agreement (as compared with the more traditional language text exercise of putting one line under the subject and two under the predicate) is to show children how to assemble and disassemble their own sentences. The activity can be introduced by having children close their eyes and visualize a sentence, such as, "The wind whipped." Then ask them to compare their visual impressions of the same sentence "dressed up" in the following manner: "On a frigid afternoon in January, the strong, biting wind whipped through the swaying, swirling branches of the towering oak tree growing on the far side of the farmer's snow-covered field." After allowing children to disassemble many sentences into their simple components in this way, let them try their hands at assembling such sentence germs as "The man cried," or "The canary warbled." For the latter sentence, the children may come up with vastly differing visions: "The arthritic old canary, having led a rich and full life in the Buddhist monastery, warbled his last tuneful notes, slipped off his perch and died"; "The peach-colored canary warbled a sweet song of love for his tiny mate, then died of a broken heart when she heard that he had been given to his owner's sister." When sharing assembled sentences, discuss the differences in visions from one sentence to the next. This routine practice of assembling and disassembling sentences will not only promote an appreciation for the richness of our language and the utter power of words, but will also lead to an intuitive understanding of grammar. Moreover, used daily, children grow in their desire and ability to write more finely-shaded sentences.

Finally, word games such as Scrabble and crossword puzzles can become lifelong habits that foster a love of words. In a similar vein, the following word games are guaranteed to provide positive experiences with words for even the most reluctant students:

• **Hinky Pinky.** A "hinky pinky" consists of two rhyming words that must be discovered by figuring out the meaning of a cryptic, two-word clue. Example: "A fatter arachnid" would be a "wider spider." Children very much enjoy doing this activity, especially in groups of three or four or as an overnight assignment for which the dictionary may be consulted, or parents involved if they wish. (Many parents have told me that this was the most "academic" fun they had ever had with their children!) Not only does this activity offer an enjoyable experience with words, but also a realistic need for the dictionary, as well as a better understanding of synonyms and their use. The following ten hinky pinkies—my favorites—can be used for an introductory contest; later children can be encouraged to devise their own for other classmates to decipher.

   1)   foul-smelling jam: smelly jelly.
   2)   an evil pastor: sinister minister.
   3)   a citrus bell: lime chime.
   4)   decayed material: rotten cotton.
   5)   an ebony slit: black crack.
   6)   a facile acne: simple pimple.
   7)   a clever elf: bright sprite.
   8)   a gaunt horse: bony pony.
   9)   an unclear pestilence: vague plague.
 10)   an abrupt pocketbook: terse purse.

• **Twisted Stories.** Twisted stories (also called "Mad Libs," which are available commercially) are "blind" stories that the children can help the teacher to write by providing some of the words. To do this activity the teacher does not show the story to the children so that they, without the benefit of the context of the story, shout out specific parts of speech as they are solicited by the teacher, while he writes them down in the appropriate spaces. Then the finished story is read aloud to the entire class. After the teacher has initiated a few of these Twisted Stories, a greater benefit comes from having the children write their own stories, making blank spaces to be filled in by their classmates. A possible story to use to introduce this activity is included here, along with the final "product." The blank spaces were filled in by members of a fourth-grade class:

The Vacation

Last summer I traveled to (city or country) <u>Japan</u> with (person) <u>Clint Eastwood</u> and (person) <u>Abe Lincoln</u> to see as many (adjective) <u>gross</u> (plural noun) <u>erasers</u> as we could find. It was a/an (adjective) <u>flimsy</u> trip. We packed enough (articles of clothing) <u>socks</u> to stay (number) <u>103</u> days. One day we visited the famous (adjective) <u>Sneaky</u> (noun) <u>Bubblegum</u> State Park. It was there I saw my first (adjective) <u>silly</u> (color) <u>purple</u> (noun) <u>pencil sharpener</u>. I took a picture of the (animals) <u>snakes</u>. They're so (adjective) <u>joyful</u>! I bought a souvenir tee-shirt that said, (adjective) "<u>Moldy</u> (plural noun) <u>books</u> love (color) <u>pink</u> (liquid) <u>milk</u>." Later we went to a ball game. The (animals) <u>cats</u> played the (number) <u>62</u>'ers. It was very (emotion) <u>sad</u>. The game was very (adjective) <u>stubborn</u>. But we had to leave (adverb) <u>gently</u> because I said, (exclamation) "<u>Holy Cow!</u>" to a (noun) <u>garbage can</u>. On the last night of our trip we went to a (type of music) <u>rock 'n' roll</u> concert. The well-known band, (adjective) <u>Interesting</u> (noun) <u>Finger</u> was on stage. I saw one musician (verb) <u>vacuum</u> his (musical instrument) <u>clarinet</u> using his (body part) <u>lung</u>. I was so (emotion) <u>jealous</u> that I bought a (noun) <u>banana</u> and mailed it home. My vacation taught me one lesson: Never give a (noun) <u>stethoscope</u> to a (adjective) <u>rad</u> (noun) <u>mouse</u>!

● **Semantic Gradient.** Another, more direct way, to encourage a discussion about words is via the use of a semantic gradient. With this device two opposite words, such as "happy" and "sad"; "small" and "large"; or "good" and "bad" are presented to children. The children must then decide what words might go between them and beyond them, and where exactly on the gradient they would go. For example, one second-grade group of youngsters came up with this list for "good" and "bad":

perfect
excellent
good
okay
mischievous
awful
bad
evil

When using such a device, it is important to tell children that there are no absolute "right" or "wrong" answers. Indeed, from a learning point of view, the process of brainstorming the words and the ensuing discussion about the relative shades of meaning is much more important than the culminating list. As the dictionary offers no "conclusive" evidence, children must build a case for their word's placement by offering reasons why they feel one word is more or less intense than another.

Fostering Positive Associations with the Dictionary

The dictionary is quite a complex reference tool without which many readers and writers would undoubtedly be lost. Many adults (I count myself among them) who read and write frequently will readily admit that they still look up several words a week through their routine contact with print. Because the dictionary can be so helpful in helping children learn to communicate more effectively, we must make certain that they feel comfortable using it. The use of the dictionary requires a hierarchy of abilities: children must first be taught to 1) locate the words, which are arranged in alphabetical order; 2) understand how to use the pronunciation guides if they are to use the word orally, and 3) find the appropriate meaning of the word. Moreover, it is simply not sufficient to teach children to rely on superficial verbalizations for words that are prompted when they are asked to memorize isolated word lists. A child, for example, who has remembered by rote that "frantic" means "wild" may then try to tell how he was picking "frantic flowers," and a child who has learned that "athletic" means "strong" might tell you about pouring "athletic vinegar" on her salad!

Rather than providing meaningless word lists and demanding that children always look up unfamiliar words, dictionary games can help children acquire a feeling of confidence and ease with the dictionary, while making it much more likely that the use of this important tool becomes a habit.

I have found the following motivational games very successful for building positive attitudes toward the dictionary. The practice afforded by such games automatically reinforces children's ability to perform the rudimentary skills just mentioned.

● **What Would You Do With It?** From the dictionary, select a word that is probably unfamiliar to your students. Write the word on the blackboard and solicit hunches about the word's use. For example, the word "freshet" is written on the blackboard and pronounced. The children are told that the word is a noun, or the name of a person, place, or thing. Then children are asked what they would do with a "freshet." Answers may range from "hang it in my closet, because it is probably a sweet smelling bag of herbs" to "step on it, because it's probably an insect of some sort." After all who want to have guessed, allow all of the children to look up the word. Children will be surprised and amused to find that a "freshet" is a flooded stream and will want to compare their hunches with the actual definition.

● **Camouflage.** This game combines motivational dictionary practice with non-threatening extemporaneous speaking and oral creativity. To introduce the game, the teacher must first explain what the word "camouflage" means and then tell children that to play this game, they must camouflage, or hide, a word. Then give children slips of paper, each of which contains a word that is just above children's oral (speaking) vocabularies; that is, words that they would not use in their everyday conversations. Ask them not to show their words to anyone else, but encourage them to consult a dictionary to get a broad feeling of the word's meaning. Next, either demonstrate yourself, or select a confident and easily verbal risk-taker to go first. Have another member of the class volunteer to ask the child a very general question, such as, "What is your favorite thing to do?" or, perhaps, "Would you rather live in this country or China?" After considering the question for a few seconds, the first child must then loosely answer the question, trying to sneak in the word that was on the slip of paper. An obvious strategy is to utilize all the "big" words that the child can think of in answer to the question in order to throw the other children off. When the child is finished answering the question, other members of the class try to guess which word was being camouflaged. The first child "wins" if the number of children who guess the camouflaged word is fewer than the sum total of incorrect guesses.

• **Clue.** The game "Password" is very popular with children and has great merit in giving children practice in thinking about the meaning of words. Unfortunately, only five can play the traditional version of this game at one time. A variation of this game, suitable for the whole class, is "Clue." One child is selected to sit facing the front of the classroom with a word that she has not seen taped to her back. Other children are put into two teams and, armed with student dictionaries, take turns offering one-word synonyms that they hope will cause the child to guess the word. As words are offered, they are written on the blackboard so that the child who is guessing can try to synthesize all the definitions that the other children have contributed. The team that says the clue that causes the child to say the word wins the round.

• **Torture the Teacher.** Often the reason children are intimidated by the dictionary is because it is so full of words they don't know, but somehow feel they should know. They feel somewhat comforted when they realize that no one knows ALL the words in the dictionary...not even their teacher! Using an unabridged dictionary, let children on a daily basis, take turns hunting for a word for which they think you might not know the meaning. For their part, they must provide the word, its pronunciation, and its part of speech. You, then, must give a reasonably accurate sense of what the word means. If you do know the word's meaning, you win for the day. If you don't know the meaning of the word, they win, and they feel smug and most pleased with themselves. Warning: this activity is NOT for the insecure!

• **Farkle.** When children become familiar enough with the peculiar stilted language of dictionary definitions, Farkle can be a fun way to practice dictionary skills while fostering creativity at the same time. To do this, select a word that is probably unknown to the class. On the blackboard, write the word, its part of speech, and its pronunciation using diacritical marking. Example: pur-lieu (per'loo), n. Then ask the children, using their imaginations, to create a definition for this word on a slip of paper using their best imitation of dictionary language. Meanwhile, the teacher writes out the actual dictionary definition on a slip of paper. Slips of paper are then collected, shuffled, and numbered. Then all the definitions are read to the class once so that class members can hear all the definitions and try to determine which is the real one. Then the definitions are read a second time and children "vote" for the one definition they think is the actual one. When the voting is completed, all children look up the word to find its true definition. The made-up definition that received the most votes wins.

• **What's the Good Word?** This game is fascinating for both children and adults because it forces one to see the essence of an object. Children are divided into small cooperative groups. The name of a very common object or item is written on the chalkboard or overhead. The teacher should choose such mundane items as: ceiling, glass, plant, board, floor, picture, etc. Children must discuss with their groups ONE word that would definitely be used in the definition for the item (caveat: this is more difficult than it appears!). Groups who guess correctly receive a group point. The game continues until a group attains five points.

• **Guide Words.** The concept of guide words is difficult for children, and plying them with workbook pages that ask them to use the guide words has met with little success. This simple game, also played in cooperative groups, asks children to write down all the words they can think of that would be on two pages of a dictionary that contains two guide words selected by the teacher (spelling doesn't count!). The group that comes up with the most words—confirmed by consulting a dictionary—wins.

Final Axioms for Guiding Growth in Vocabulary

The underlying supposition in an Affective Language Arts program is that learning to communicate should be rewarding and enjoyable; the vocabulary-building activities just described will certainly help make it so. But because I have recently seen so many routine classroom practices that could seriously dampen this enthusiasm, I would like to offer a few words of caution here:

1) DO NOT consistently tell children to look up words they don't know or can't spell. For spelling purposes, it is better to just show the child how to spell the word, or let him try to sound it out, to be edited at a later time. For meaning purposes, at times just tell the child what the word means. Also, encourage children to keep personal VIP word books in which they write down any unfamiliar words which they have encountered in school or while reading at home. Later, when they have accumulated 10-15 such words, they can look them up all at once. Encourage them to share some of the VIP words that they especially like with the rest of the class.

2) DO NOT give children words to memorize that have been taken from commercial word lists. Words memorized in isolation have little meaning or interest to children and will soon be forgotten. The words that children readily want to learn and have the best chance of remembering come from topics they are

currently studying or, even better yet, words for which they have expressed an interest in knowing themselves.

3) DO NOT give children simple synonyms for words. Instead offer them the whole sense of what the word means, moving from the general to the specific, and telling them what the word is like and what the word is unlike compared with that which they already know. For example, to explain the word "sword" you might say that it is something to cut with, like a knife, but much sharper and bigger; but unlike a knife, it is usually used as a weapon.

4) DO NOT use the dictionary as a "tutor" for students learning English as a second language. I have been in too many classrooms where a child who speaks little or no English is put by himself in the back of the classroom to "learn English" by copying dictionary pages. Not only does he learn to despise the dictionary, but by being segregated from the rest of the class he is denied the language interaction that is the best possible environment in which to acquire a second language.

5) DO NOT use the dictionary as a punishment. As much as I would like to believe that this final caveat goes without saying, I am still observing practices in otherwise fine school districts where children are instructed to copy whole pages from dictionaries as punishment for minor rule infractions! Besides the fact that the punishment has nothing to do with the "crime," the practice will very quickly counteract any positive feelings that have been connected with the dictionary.

Summary

The affective teacher of language arts can joyfully capitalize on the fact that it is in the nature of the child to love words and word play. If she can then simply take advantage of the myriad of occasions during the day when children are directing their own language through play, she can quite naturally integrate vocabulary development into the entire curriculum.

The teacher can also plan special experiences for children that can be presented in such an interesting and inviting way that children will begin to appreciate the various shades of meaning possible in our language, the interesting ways that words relate to one another, and how the dictionary can become a liberating tool that will allow independent investigation of words. A host of activities leading to these ends have been presented in this chapter. In a classroom where words are exciting for both the teacher and the students, great things often happen. Just the right word is eagerly sought to convey an intense feeling or a physical description; sentences, too, are now designed to create a precise message or personal vision. Children begin to understand that if they think something, they can say it or write it. It is indeed a revelation to children when they first see that they will soon have the very tools at their command to communicate clearly what is in their hearts and minds. The key to a more dynamic interaction with the rest of the world is within their grasp.

Chapter Nine

Visualization Activities: Why the Book Was Better Than the Movie

There is probably a good reason for the often heard cliche, "It was a great movie, but the book was even better!" Most people who really do enjoy reading use the incredible resource of their own imaginations while reading a good book. They actively bring their own myriad of life's experiences to the text, allowing their minds to vividly color the characters and events exactly the way they wish them to be. The text comes alive for them in the most personal and intense kind of way. No wonder the film—always a far cry from what the fertile imagination has conjured—is a disappointment to them!

In today's high-tech world, the old cliché is not heard as often among young people and I worry that we are short-changing them by taking away the imaginative challenges in their recreational activities. Instead of children making up a fanciful dialogue with their teddy bears, for example, the toys can now instigate and control sophisticated "conversations," while video games have become so frighteningly graphic that virtually nothing needs to be imagined. Even popular songs now provide lavishly-produced videos, dismissing the need for youngsters to call up any of their own images to make the lyrics come alive.

Because children are being given fewer and fewer opportunities to use their imaginations naturally, it becomes crucial to include visualization activities in an Affective Language Arts program. For one thing, when children are in the midst of the writing process they must be able to consult their own personal "mind pictures" to decide what should come next in their work. Visualization exercises can strengthen this ability, making it almost second-nature to children. As a result, they become more confident and capable writers.

Additionally, encouraging children to actively visualize words and concepts may not only help them to enjoy reading more thoroughly, but it can also improve their understanding of what they read. As an example, a program focusing on the skill of using visual imagery was implemented in the Escondido Union School District. Gains in comprehension were shown that were over three times that of previous years (Escondido Union School District, 1979).

The following chapter will give the affective teacher specific steps, guidelines, and visualization activities that can be used as motivational pre-writing prompts and will also help children to glean more pleasure from reading by becoming better able to use their imaginations to appreciate sensory and descriptive imagery. Additionally, the chapter will describe some ways teachers can familiarize their students with the metacognitive strategy of turning to their own personal mind pictures for guidance when writing.

Guidelines for Using Visualization

To obtain the optimal affective benefits from the routine use of visualizing, the sensitive teacher may want to keep in mind the following general guidelines (Fredericks, 1986):

1)   Children first need to be reassured that there are no "correct" or "incorrect" mind pictures; whatever their imaginations dictate are valid responses.

2)   Children must learn to respect each other's mind pictures, understanding that the images that pop into one's mind are often influenced by one's own past experiences.

3)   Children need enough "wait time" to bring forth their images. If they are rushed, some children will draw blanks and begin to believe that their imaginations are somehow inadequate.

4)   Allow sufficient time to discuss images in a supportive, cooperative and informal atmosphere that conveys the feeling to children that everyone's images are worth exploring.

5)   Help children to develop the skill of elaboration by actively seeking details about their contributions. For example,

if a child offers, "I see a blue house," the teacher might reply, "Oh—that's interesting. Can you tell us more about the blue house?"

Activities to Foster Visualization

For some fluent children, visualization comes quite naturally, and they write prolifically without interruption. Others may need practice creating images in their minds as a precursor to writing.

Mundell (1985) has presented a process for helping children to more actively use their imaginations:

1)   **Give children practice visualizing concrete objects.** Allow children the opportunity to look very carefully at everyday objects, such as the pencil sharpener, a favorite toy, or their tennis shoes. Have them close their eyes and try to recreate every detail of the object in their minds, and then with their eyes open, compare their mental image with the actual object. Finally, let them verbally or pictorially try to recreate the object, attempting to include even those details they had overlooked the first time.

For an added oral language dimension to the previous exercise, have one child select an object and put it in a bag so that it is out of sight to the other members of the class. Let the child describe all the visual attributes of the object that would help the other children identify it while the others try to draw the object from the child's description. Then compare the object with the children's drawings and discuss the reasons for the sometimes humorous discrepancies between the drawings and the actual object.

A "human" variation of this activity is to select a child to leave the classroom for a few moments. Have the rest of the children in the class describe the absent child by trying to visualize everything the absent child was wearing, and his or her height, weight, and eyes and hair color. When the child reenters the classroom compare the class members' visual memory with the child's actual appearance.

2)   **Give children practice recalling scenes or experiences from outside the classroom.** To help children become more accurate observers, ask them to close their eyes and picture their family car (or pet, or living room, etc.). As they are thinking about it, orally "walk" them around the outside of the car, telling them to try to imagine the wheels, the hub caps, the doors (two or four?), the color of the paint, the grille, the license plates, etc. Next, have the children draw a picture of the car with as much detail as they can remember. Then ask them to take their drawings home and compare them with the actual vehicles.

Every child has watched a helium-filled balloon go up into the sky until it is out of sight. Key into this experience common to children by showing them the film *The Red Balloon*. Then follow the viewing with the reading aloud of Shel Silverstein's poem "Eight Balloons" while children close their eyes (this poem describes the journey of eight balloons whose sad fates range from landing on a frying pan to entering a crocodile's mouth). Ask the children to now imagine that they are holding their own helium-filled balloons which suddenly escape into the air. Give them a few moments to image the flight of their balloons and then encourage them to give an oral or pictorial account of the balloon's journey.

Finally, to demonstrate to children how their visual and olfactory memories combine to create even stronger memories, bring in several items with strong aromas without revealing to the children what they are. Have the children close their eyes and sniff the items whose smell usually evokes explicit memories of past experiences, such as leather, pine cones, a plastic doll, bubble gum, or lavender sachet. Ask children to then share the mental images that come to their minds of people or places that they may associate with these scents (Cecil and Lauritzen, 1994).

3)   **Give children practice listening to high imagery stories and relating them to their own experiences.** Read stories aloud to children that contain a great deal of visual imagery, such as the books *Tuck Everlasting* or *Julie of the Wolves*. Stop every so often and allow children to share their

mental images of how the characters, settings, or events have come to life in their minds.

Also, do "mental adventure" exercises on a routine basis. While having children close their eyes, orally give them a guided imagery of a situation such as a safari in deepest Africa or a tamer adventure, like a walk in the forest:

"Picture yourself in a forest. You are strolling among the trees on a well-worn path. What is the weather like? (Pause to let children imagine.) As you walk along, you see a person. You exchange glances with the person, and then that person runs quickly in the other direction. Why? (Pause.) You continue walking and soon come to a body of water. What is it? How deep, how wide, how cold? (Pause.) You cross it—how? (Pause.) You find the path again on the other side and begin walking again. Soon you almost trip on a cup lying in the middle of the path. You stoop to pick it up and examine it carefully. What does it look like? (Pause.) You put it down. Why? (Pause.) You keep walking until the path leads to a fence. You climb over the fence and see a house. What does the house look like? (Pause.) You enter the house and find yourself in the kitchen. What is the kitchen like? (Pause.) You sit down at the kitchen table and see that there is something interesting on the table. What is it? (Pause.) While you are looking at it, the person whom you saw in the forest walks into the kitchen. Describe him or her."

Ask the children to then retrace their individual journeys orally for the class or, at later stages, in written form.

Allow pairs of children to act out their journeys for the rest of the class if they wish.

Another high-imagery listening experience that you can provide for your class is to have them listen to *The Adventures of Robinson Crusoe*, *The Cay*, or *Swiss Family Robinson*. Have them close their eyes and visualize their own versions of a shipwreck. Then, over the period of time during which the story is read, ask them to write a series of journal entries of their adventures on their own make-believe islands, encouraging them to "borrow" as much as they would like from the text. Let each child select his own favorite entry to dramatize into an original one-act play for the rest of the class.

Trusting Mind Pictures to Tell What Happens Next

To provide children with the "ignition key" that will always be at their disposal when they are writing independently, spontaneous story technique (SST) (Kolpakoff, 1986) can serve as the bridge between a child's pictorial imagination, oral language, and writing. This method is ideal for use at all grade levels, but requires much practice and the initial enthusiastic participation of the teacher as storyteller.

To begin using this technique, children should be gathered around the teacher in a relaxed fashion, preferably on the floor. Then the teacher instructs her students to close their eyes and make their minds as empty as possible. The rest of a typical SST exercise goes something like this:

"Now your mind is empty. But as soon as you 'see' something, raise your hand."

(The teacher then solicits responses as to what individual children have visualized and encourages elaboration.)

"Again, I want you to make your mind as empty as possible, but this time I'm going to ask you to do something very strange! When I tell you NOT to see something, try as hard as you can, NOT to see it! Now—DO NOT see a pink monster!"

(Stop and discuss with children how many of them actually did see a pink monster and have children share what their various monsters looked like. Continue in this manner with several other examples of things you tell children NOT to see.)

"Now I want you to make your mind empty once more and hold it on empty for as long as you can. When a picture does come into your mind, raise your hand."

(Wait until all hands are raised and then solicit the children's images. Praise effective elaboration that allows other children to "see," too.)

"I am now going to ask you to put your last picture back in your mind again. Hold that picture there as long as you can. When that picture goes away or changes to a new picture, please raise your hand."

(When all children have new pictures, let them share them.)

After a number of SST sessions, when children have become much more confident about using their imaginations and are willingly sharing their images, they are ready to begin to use these visual skills to problem-solve endings to stories. They can now be assured that they can **always** know what comes next in a story; all they have to do is to allow their minds to create the next picture. At this stage, the teacher will want to have a session include a "cliff-hanger" story told first by the teacher, but in later sessions, made up by student volunteers. A cliff-hanger story might go like this:

"Close your eyes and let your mind be empty. Now I want you to picture yourself entering a room in an old attic. It is raining and you can hear the soft patter of raindrops on the roof. Hear them? (Pause.) You wander around the stuffy attic and notice an old rocking horse and a stuffed rabbit with an ear missing. You walk toward a broken window and see a large spider web. The spider suddenly swoops down to look at you (pause for squeals from the squeamish), and then scurries quickly away. Your eye catches a large mirror on the far wall of the attic. It has fancy gold decorations on all sides and is covered with several layers of dust. You move over to it and start to brush off some of the dust when you discover, to your surprise, that you can walk through the mirror. You push your body through the mirror and you see..."

At this critical point, ask children to open their eyes and share their visions of what was on the other side of the mirror.

Other visualization stories that could be expanded and used in a similar way are these:

● "You are exploring a deep, dark cave. You suddenly hear a strong, frightening voice. You try to find your way back to the entrance, but it seems that all the rooms in the cave look very much alike. You panic as you realize the voice is coming closer and closer. Suddenly, you see who it is . . ."

● "You are flying in an airplane over some cornfields in the Midwest. Suddenly the engine starts to sputter and the plane begins to lose altitude. You decide to bail out and so you quickly put on your parachute. You are as scared as you have ever been, but you jump out of the plane, and . . ."

● "You are skindiving off the coast of Australia. You are having fun playing hide and seek with the groupers and friendly parrot fish. Suddenly you spy an old abandoned ship and you dive down to explore it. You open the door to the captain's quarters and are amazed to find..."

When children are feeling confident that they now can "know" what will happen next in a story through their mind pictures, they are ready to begin using story boards to help them finish the rest of their stories. The "story board" for very young children is simply a piece of paper divided into six panels on which children pictorially sequence the next six events in the story. For older children, the panels are the next six pages of text.

Individual tape recorders are sometimes useful to help children make the transition from "mind pictures" to the oral telling of incidents, to the written version. With the tape recorder, the children can revise and expand their text until they are completely satisfied with their story before writing anything. Then they can use their recording to help them transcribe the text onto paper, continually checking with their mind pictures for any new information.

While the children are busy writing, the teacher's role is to interact with his students in a non-directive way to help them to work through their writing problems and temporary blocks. Kolpakoff suggests three specific interactive techniques that can enable the teacher to become a more effective writing facilitator:

1)   **Marking time.** When children tell the teacher that they don't know what comes next, the teacher may deliberately NOT respond to this lament and, instead, distract the child from the

writing task by instigating a very brief chat about something totally unrelated to the child's current writing. This chance for the child to "get away" from the intensity of creating for a few seconds often allows that child to then get back to her writing with fresh ideas and immediate inspiration—a ploy used often by professional writers.

2) **Next picture.** When a child is "stuck," another technique is to read the child's work and then offer a snippet of an idea which could lead to a new set of possibilities. For example, a child writing about the mirror in the attic may be blocked when he sees a picnic area on the other side of the mirror, but can't get an idea what happens there. The teacher might suggest, "I see a little boy running away from his parents into the woods and..." At that point the teacher smiles and walks away, promising to check back later to see how the author is doing.

3) **Writer's talk.** Because the teacher is ordinarily so engrossed in her role of support person, often the only real intellectual interchange between teacher and young author is of the offer to help or request for assistance variety. Another important role for the teacher when children are writing from their imaginations is simply to talk to each child, author to author, making respectful comments about each one's imaginative thoughts and ideas. Teachers are then able to be perceived as helpful collaborators rather than "powerful beings with all the answers."

Visualization across the Curriculum
The skill of visualizing should have a prominent place in many areas of a whole language elementary curriculum, where the language arts are thoroughly integrated, especially when abstract concepts and ideas need to be made more concrete and meaningful for the younger child. Social studies, for example, requires children to do much writing of an analytical/expository nature, but when guided imagery is used to mentally "walk" children through the content areas, children can become more

personally involved through the sensory/descriptive information that visualization provides for them.

Sprowl (1986) uses the image of present, familiar situations to help children relate to difficult and abstract concepts. For example, to show children how technology has affected their lives, he asks them to close their eyes and imagine that it is early morning and they are in the bathroom trying to get ready for school. He then has them mentally take away any machines that they would normally use, such as electric toothbrushes, hair dryers or electric rollers. Of course, there is no light in the bathroom. Next he has them picture themselves walking to their bedroom, erasing the images of their radio or stereo, or even any clothing that was made by machine. On the way to the kitchen they pass through the living room and the children are told it is now bereft of the telephone, television, VCR, and again, lights. The children must then try to imagine their kitchen without the stove, refrigerator, washer, dryer, or dishwasher. Finally, children are instructed to do away with even the walls and the carpets, as these items, too, are made by machines.

Because this mental voyage is so graphic and personal for children, they truly begin to understand, in a very memorable way, the concept of a world without the modern technology that they quite naturally take for granted. Such guided imagery can also be used to effectively introduce other important global concepts such as poverty, racism, nuclear war, or life in another country, to name just a few.

Summary

Visualization activities invest children with the ability to look inside themselves to "see" stories more clearly and to trust that their own minds will know what should happen next for their own creations. The skill is a fundamental technique that should be at the core of any affective language arts program, for it quite clearly demonstrates to children that they must be active, rather than passive, participants in their own development as writers. Visualization gives them, also, one more important tool that will allow them to communicate effectively. It is a tool that almost all children naturally possess, but somehow, somewhere, it is often discarded in deference to other external demands that are placed upon them.

This chapter offers guidelines for using visualization activities in the classroom and includes a variety of fun exercises to help children relearn this important skill. By so doing, children's writing, thinking, and enjoyment of reading will be positively impacted. More importantly, children will no longer have to be dependent upon the teacher to help them make decisions about "what should come next" in their writing. Through the tremendous power of their fertile imaginations, children will most likely be delighted to find that a whole army of wonderful ideas is very much alive somewhere in their minds, patiently waiting to be invited onto the page.

References

Cecil, N.L. and P. Lauritzen. "Visualization: The Ignition Key." *Literacy and the Arts in the Integrated Classroom: Alternative Ways of Knowing*. White Plains, NY: Longman, 1994.

Escondido Union School District. *Mind's Eyes—Creating Mental Pictures from Pirated Words*. Escondido, CA: Escondido Union School District Board of Education, 1979.

Fredericks, A. "Mental Imagery Activities to Improve Comprehension." *The Reading Teacher* 40 (October 1986): pp. 78-81.

Kolpakoff, I. "Spontaneous Story Technique." Unpublished manuscript, 1986.

Mundell, D.D. *Mental Imagery: Do You See What I Say?* Oklahoma City, OK: Oklahoma State Department of Education, 1985.

Pressley, G.M. "Mental Imagery Helps Eight Year Olds Remember What They Read." *Journal of Educational Psychology* 68, No. 4, (1976): pp. 355-59.

Sprowl, D. "Guided Imagery in the Social Studies." *Practical Ideas for Teaching Writing as a Process*. Sacramento, CA: California State Department of Education, 1986.

Chapter Ten

Role-Playing: Trying Life on for Size

In one classroom, a small boy is very hungry and watches while others eat voraciously, then smiles gratefully when a little girl shyly offers him half of her sandwich. In another classroom, a child proudly explains to her peers how she helped hundreds of slaves escape to freedom using the underground railroad. A glimpse into a third classroom finds a little girl leaving home for an exciting land far, far away, wondering if she'll ever again see her parents.

Transported by the evocative magic of role playing, these children put themselves in the places of other people. In so doing, they begin to learn how it feels to be someone else. Role plays like these, when used as tools in an Affective Language Arts program, can open a child's eyes to see and her heart to listen and understand.

The term "role playing" is used to refer to a type of play-acting in the classroom. By definition, it is a dramatic oral language activity in which children explore, in the most intimate way, the relationships of human living for the purpose of acquiring needed understandings and intrapersonal communication skills. But unlike children's free play, which is unstructured, role playing can occur under a teacher's guidance. Yet, unlike the more formally structured "drama" in which set lines are read or memorized, role playing unfolds rather spontaneously, without a predetermined script. It uses the dramatic elements of characterization and dialogue. Empathy is unusually intense in a role play because the actor is attempting to take on the internal characteristics of the person she is fashioning.

In the elementary classroom, role plays can grow out of current daily situations, problems, past episodes, or concepts that have implications for learning in the content areas. Sometimes the actual situation itself is the point of departure; other times, the teacher arranges the environment. Still another approach is to bring to life a beloved children's story in which there are relationships to be understood and rich opportunities for characterization.

But whether the point of departure is a real life experience, an important concept, a story, or a hypothetical event, the process through which learning can evolve the most dynamically is through role playing. This is the premise of this chapter: let children be actors and in acting they will learn. Let them engage in creative make-believe and they will discover what no teacher can teach them. Let them reflectively reenact arguments and they will develop insight and problem-solving skills. Let them simulate concepts and that which is unclear will be understood and that which is remote will become near and alive.

Role Playing to Reverse Bad Situations

Consider the following scenario that occurs daily, in various formats, on playgrounds across the country at recess:

Jimmy: I'm getting tired of playing kickball every day. Today why don't we play soccer instead?

Ryan: Nah, let's not play soccer. I don't know how to play soccer. Besides, soccer's a sissy game. Let's either play kickball or baseball.

Jason: No. I like Jimmy's idea. Let's play soccer for a change. I'll be the captain and Jimmy can be the other captain. Let's choose up sides!

Ryan: No WAY! I have the ball, and you can't have it if you're going to play soccer!

Jimmy: I'm telling the teacher on you, you creep!

Ryan: Go ahead! She'll take my side!

Jason: All right, just give me the ball RIGHT NOW, or I'm gonna beat you up!

Ryan: Oh yeah? You and whose army?!

In the next few moments, of course, the argument escalates into fisticuffs between Ryan and Jason. Normally, the situation ends with angry feelings all around, as all three boys are reprimanded and/or sent to the principal's office by the teacher on recess duty. Everyone involved is thoroughly disgruntled and little, if anything, has been learned through the ordeal. The weary teacher and the three boys then go back to the classroom, still upset about what happened, but trying to put their minds to more academic concerns.

Role playing is the vehicle through which this unfortunate scenario might have been transformed into a dynamic oral language/social science lesson, not only for the boys involved, but for the rest of the class as well. Role playing can make positive use of an event that has just occurred, or even one that is fictitious, and make it immediately come alive for children to act out, and then think about and discuss. The activity can help children to consider the variety of alternative solutions available for handling problems and it can provide a deeper understanding about what causes crises to occur and what the effects are likely to be.

If a teacher wanted the children to gain insight from the aforementioned scenario, for example, he would need to guide his students through these steps:

1) Have a neutral observer from the class give his or her version of what happened;

2) Select children to play the roles of each person involved;

3) Ask the actors to take a few moments to prepare two skits: the first an actual reenactment of the situation as it actually happened, and a second skit that changes the outcome to a more positive, alternative ending to the conflict;

4) While the actors are preparing their skits, instruct the other children to, "Watch what the actors do and say. Try to put yourselves in their shoes and feel what they must be feeling. As you are watching, be thinking of some other ways in which the conflict could have been resolved."

5) Have the actors present their skits in the center of the classroom, surrounded by the other class members;

6) In sequence, reflect upon the differences in the two skits. Encourage other class members to contribute their alternative solutions to the problem;

7) Finally, discuss the "cause" and "effect" patterns in the two skits in terms of words or actions and resultant feelings.

For this particular playground scenario, Jason and Ryan, the two children who were involved in the original altercation, might be asked to play themselves in the reenactment or, to develop more insight into each other's point of view, they could also be asked to switch roles. The two boys' alternative solution to the conflict might turn out to be Jason conceding that they will play kick ball again, as they always do. Other class members who have watched both skits as dispassionate observers may have some different suggestions for them: Since Ryan has admitted that he doesn't know how to play soccer, why don't Jason and Jimmy teach him how to play? Or, why don't they set up a rotating schedule of playing kick ball one day, baseball the following day and soccer the next? Or, what would happen if they were to agree to toss a coin each day to decide which game was to be played?

Finally, through a guided reflective discussion, all the children in the class can begin to see exactly what turn of events caused the build-up of bad feelings that resulted in two friends having a fist fight. More importantly, they have themselves problem-solved some ways to lessen the chances of the unfortunate situation from recurring.

Role Playing Fictitious Events
While it is always a good idea to "catch the moment" in order to turn a bad situation into a good one, as in the previously mentioned scenario, it is also of great benefit to role play hypothetical situations to ward off certain problems **before** they occur. By being "tuned in" to certain age-related behavioral characteristics, the affective teacher can help children consider

in advance certain situations that can often cause conflict. Consider these common scenes from elementary classroom life:

1) Cheryl, Jennifer, and Lisa are talking about Brittany's pajama party which is coming up on the weekend. Shirley strolls over to them and asks what is happening. At first they don't answer, but she presses them, so they tell her about the party, to which they know she would never be invited. Shirley blurts out, "Will you ask Brittany if I could come too?" The other girls just laugh at Shirley. She gets angry and calls them names.

2) Lunch money is missing from Zack's desk. Three boys, John, Mark, and Jesse say they know who took it, but they are afraid to tell. Zack confronts Mark and tells him if he doesn't tell who took his money, he will beat him up. Mark names an innocent child, Tam, who gives Zack his own lunch money and cries the rest of the day.

3) David's father has been sent to prison. A group of boys, Kevin, Josh, and Tim, taunt him about it, saying that his father is a murderer and a thief and David must be bad, too. David retaliates by making up lies about Kevin's mother, vowing to hurt Tim's little brother, and tripping Josh as he gets out of his seat. At recess, the three boys beat David up.

4) Returning to the room from lunch, Denise cannot find her pencil. She cries out in a loud voice, "WHO STOLE MY PENCIL?" When no one answers her question, she turns to Billy, who sits behind her, and takes one of the pencils from on top of his desk. "Hey...that's MY pencil!" Billy yells, and the two stage a heated tug-of-war over the pencil.

Having children act out the above situations and then reflect upon possible solutions provides an excellent forum for the verbalizations of their opinions, attitudes and emerging values. Additionally, consistent role playing of these and similar situations that they may soon encounter leads to four positive outcomes in the classroom:

1) The common problems of human interaction are personalized and made concrete so that children can clearly look

at them and learn to proactively communicate their feelings about them;

2) When the entire class is involved in reflecting on possible alternative solutions, each student begins to take personal responsibility for **all** problems that arise in the class;

3) Sometimes problems are actually resolved before they ever occur through the group interaction and joint verbal commitments to solutions;

4) Finally, children come to understand that satisfactory solutions and positive changes in behavior are generally brought about through thoughtful discussion, rather than through impulsive reacting or aggression.

Role Playing Characters in Children's Literature

When reading a book with many complex characters to a group of elementary children, role playing can help make the characters in the book come alive and help children to discover the relationship between what they are reading and their own lives.

This role playing of literature can be used with many favorite children's stories, such as *Peter Pan*. First of all, students work in pairs so that every child is involved. Partners are assigned, rather than allowing students to choose their own, to make sure that shy children are paired with more outgoing ones. Each pair of children is assigned one role as a character or to the author, or adaptor. The characters to be assigned for *Peter Pan*, for example, might be these:

Author	Wendy	Mrs. Darling
Captain Hook	Peter Pan	John
Mr. Darling	(1) pirate	Tinker Bell
Michael	Nana	the crocodile

After reading the story, all the children are then asked to study the text in light of their own character's personality and motivation during every part of the text. To clarify confusing points, pairs should be encouraged to consult the teacher as character to reader or reader to reader.

For the second part of the project, each pair draws up a list of questions—at least one question for each of the other characters in the book and one for the author. The questions might be those a reader would ask about the story, or even those a character might ask another character. Also, children should be urged to include some questions that go beyond the scope of the book, such as, "Peter, do you ever see Wendy anymore now that she's grown up?" or "Pirate, what do you think your punishment would have been for making people walk the plank if you had been caught?"

After this preparation has been completed, the children are ready for the role playing. Each pair wears character name tags so that class members will have no problem identifying the character they wish to question. Members of each pair take turns answering questions, although they are free to collaborate.

The teacher opens the session by asking the pair on her right the first question, "Mrs. Darling, how did you feel when you first learned that your children were gone from the nursery?" Then the children go around the circle, asking a question of a different character each time, unless someone wants to ask a follow-up question related to the previous one, such as, "If you were so sad about losing your children, Mrs. Darling, why didn't you call the police or the FBI?"

At first, expect the questions and answers to be somewhat stilted. Children may initially ask obvious, factual questions eliciting responses that rely solely on textual information, like, "Captain Hook, who cut off your hand?" As they get more into the spirit of role playing, however, they begin to ask more probing questions that get them interacting in more personal ways. For instance, Peter Pan might be asked, "Can you explain why it is that you don't want to grow up?" to which Peter might reply, "As a child, I can always do just exactly as I wish and fly around having fun. If I don't grow up I will never have to go out and get a job."

Another child counteracts with, "But won't it make you sad when all of your friends grow up and then you have no one to play with? I felt kind of like that when my sister got married and moved away!"

Similar role plays can be used with any number of children's books that contain a large cast of interesting characters that in some way reflect real life. Children not only gain a deeper appreciation of the characters and new insight into themselves, but they can actually bring the whole story to life, investigating one another's feelings and motives. At times they find themselves becoming frustrated, puzzled, and even angry, but always enlightened by the characters, who have become infinitely more memorable.

Role Playing Mock Debates and Interviews

Some years ago, Steve Allen used to host a program called "Meeting of the Minds" on which he would interview actors and actresses who would be playing the part of certain serious personalities of the past, such as Marie Curie or Sigmund Freud. A fascinating discussion would take place as Steve asked his pretend guests all those probing kinds of questions that we would like to ask those persons if they were alive in today's world.

Children, too, will thoroughly enjoy similar role plays in the classroom. Such an activity becomes a self-motivating reason to do historical research because such labor will, in this instance, lead to an exciting and challenging chance to become, for a while, a very famous person.

To prepare for the presentation, pairs of children must decide on a character from history, preferably one who is somewhat familiar to the other members of the class. The pair must then research the person thoroughly—using a wide spectrum of media including videos, if available—so that they can become acquainted with the facts of the person's life, significant events, his or her personality or style of dress, opinions or political orientations, mannerisms, accent, and perhaps even memorize some of the quotations for which the person is best known. Among the historical figures who will work well for this activity would be:

Albert Einstein	Will Rogers	Mahatma Gandhi
Eleanor Roosevelt	Jesse Owens	Albert Schweitzer
Martin L. King, Jr.	Walt Disney	Abraham Lincoln
Harriette Tubman	Clara Barton	Amelia Earhart
John F. Kennedy	Paul Revere	King George III

Next, from the research the pair will draw up a list of provocative questions that would ask the historical figure to project how he or she would respond to current world issues or events. For example, Abraham Lincoln might be asked, "What are your thoughts on apartheid?" and his response would be largely based upon what the two researchers have discovered about Lincoln's contributions to the abolition of slavery, as well as their general understanding of the man's values.

For the presentation, the pair would decide who would play the part of the historical figure while the other would be the interviewer and ask the prearranged questions. After the interview session, the rest of the class, who have been taking notes, would be encouraged to ask their own questions of the person while the historical person tries to "think in character," and respond as the person might actually have responded.

The follow-up discussion is a time for the teacher and the students in the "audience" to try to clear up any obvious inconsistencies in the historical figure's responses by providing documented reasons for their objections. For example, if a student playing the role of Dr. Martin Luther King, Jr., has stated that he would support the war in Nicaragua, it would be important to remind the student about the implications of King's credo of passive resistance. Most importantly, during the reflective discussion there must be ample time to share new appreciations and insight into the historical figure in his or her now human, multi-dimensional form, and to explore any new questions or concerns that were raised.

Understanding Concepts through Simulation

Sometimes in the course of teaching children it becomes clear that all the verbalization in the world is failing to get across a certain important idea. The teacher knows that the abstract concept she is trying to convey is just not making any sense to her concrete, hands-on learners. In this situation it is sometimes advisable to preplan experiences where the children can actually simulate—or vicariously play act—the concept. This acting out of an idea brings about a sense of discovery of just what the teacher is talking about as well as, in some cases, a visceral response that is not soon forgotten. Setting the stage for such a discovery often takes a good deal of time and effort, so it is therefore not feasible for every concept that is addressed. However, some concepts, such as the three described below, because of their complex nature, cannot truly be internalized by children without the total self-involvement that simulation affords.

Haves and Have Nots

Hopefully, most of the children that we teach will never have had the experience of going to bed hungry, but therefore they cannot always empathize fully with the two-thirds of the world's people who are starving. Children take for granted that their basic needs will be met and therefore grow up quite insulated from the desperate concerns of those who are more unfortunate. To give children a very basic glimpse of how inequitable it is to have the world's wealth so unevenly distributed, arrange with the school cafeteria to provide lunch for only one-third of your class for one day. For another third, bring small amounts of rice. The remaining third will have no lunch. To begin the simulation, allow children to draw straws numbered one, two, or three to determine what their lunch fare will be. Explain to them that they are taking part in a very important experiment and you will discuss the reasons later, but that they should write down all questions, feelings, and complaints that they have. There will, of course, be much moaning and groaning from those who have been given only a bowl of rice; more so from those children who have received no lunch. Make it clear to the "no lunch" group that they must not buy food from any other source, but that they may ask children with regular lunches to share, although those children are not obligated to do so. At a later time (when hunger and anger have abated), encourage the three groups of children to vent their feelings and share their written records. As the third group complains that being given nothing to eat was unfair, they are ready to hear that millions of people are starving daily. Have those children in the simulation who shared and those who received this charity share their feelings. Finally, allow children to brainstorm some things that they now feel could be done to ease world hunger.

Bartering

Economic concepts such as "supply and demand" and why money is used as an exchange medium are best conveyed through a simulation of bartering, much like people did in the days before money, as we know it, was used. For this activity, provide a variety of small toys and objects so that there are enough for each child in the class to be given five identical items. Distribute the same set of five items to several children—such as five paper clips to six children—but give sets of the more desirable items, like balloons or pencils, to only one child each. On the blackboard list all the items that have been distributed and the number of each that there are. Then tell children that they will have five minutes to trade their objects with as many other class members as they need to in order to end up with exactly what they want. When they have finished trading, ask them to sit down and recount the exchanges they had to go through to get what they have. Next ask children to orally share their bartering experiences. Some children who had items that were in abundant supply or of lesser intrinsic value (such as the paper clips) will have had a difficult time and will probably not have ended up with what they wanted. Other children, who started out with scarcer or more desirable items, will have happier tales to tell. Finally, discuss: What happened when there were too many items? What happened when someone had the most desirable items? In what way would money have made the trading easier? How do you think the worth, or value, of objects is determined?

Prejudice

Much has been written about some very intense simulations of prejudice that were carried to such an extreme that children were psychologically damaged when the teacher and perpetrators apparently began to lose touch with what was simulation and what was reality. Rest assured that a more reasoned simulation can have the desired effect without causing lasting harm.

For this simulation children need to be artificially categorized as "good" or "bad" according to some God-given trait over which they have no control, such as gender, or color of hair or eyes. If eye color is chosen, for example, children would be told that those children with brown eyes would be first to go to recess and the drinking fountain. Throughout the day they would receive many other small privileges. When children question this favoritism, tell them that brown-eyed children are receiving differential treatment because some ignorant people might believe that they are simply "better" than those with blue or green eyes. Because of the anger and frustration that this situation quite naturally produces, the activity should not continue for more than a morning or afternoon, at most. After that time, the blackboard should be divided into two columns. First have the brown-eyed children share their feelings and reactions, and then the non-brown-eyed. Tell children that while this was only a rather unhappy game, some people really do judge people on the basis of such superficial traits in real life. Discuss how people really **should** be evaluated and how this simulation might help these people who judge others on traits that they can do nothing about. Finally, ask children to elaborate on how this activity might change the way they behave toward other people in the future.

Other important concepts to be assimilated can also be understood on a deeper level by following this rudimentary framework for guiding simulation activities:

1) Strip the concept to its most basic form and decide upon what methods and materials would be most effective in getting the point across. Allow a sufficient block of time for the activity, and be sure to communicate to parents and administrators ahead of time exactly what you are trying to do.

2) With minimal explanations, have children act out the concept. Ask them to write down questions and feelings about what is going on.

3) Let children describe what happened in their own words. Explain the concept they were simulating and ask them, "What did you learn about _____?" "Who do you think might benefit from also doing this activity?" "Did you think of any new problems to be solved as a result of doing this activity?"

Summary

We know that young children are concrete, hands-on learners whose preoccupation is mainly with themselves. This should not be cause for dismay, for it is exactly in this search for self-understanding that children start to make sense of the world around them. And because this is so, there is no more effective approach to the task of teaching interpersonal communication skills than by first observing the way children orient themselves to their environment as they seek self-understanding through role playing.

Seeking to understand who they are and what their relationships to other people, situations, and concepts are, children will role play life as they see it. Using their imagination, they create make-believe worlds that, like a prism, illuminate and clarify in miniature the meanings and values they are discovering in living with other human beings. Role-playing, they push themselves out into the world of others and in so doing, take stock of their own values and ideas. Deeper insights develop as children stretch the boundaries of their own life space.

In short, through role playing children begin to try on life for size, but they do so in the relative safety of an affective classroom environment where it always fits each child perfectly.

Chapter Eleven

The Integrated Teaching Unit: Tying It All Together

Many years ago when I was doing my undergraduate work in teacher education, the "buzz word" was UNIT. The unit was touted to be THE hottest, most innovative way to teach and if you didn't know how to teach using this approach, you were led to believe that you would quickly be considered a teaching "dinosaur."

Teaching by means of the unit, which was developed in the John Dewey Schools of the late twenties and early thirties, is still alive and well today and by most accounts, considered an effective strategy for fulfilling the instructional goals of the modern elementary curriculum. It also seems suited to the objectives of an Affective Language Arts program because it so effectively encourages individual creativity and language development. Yet the field of social studies has long claimed the teaching unit as its own exclusive property. How, then, is it possible for unit teaching to serve as a vehicle through which to more expansively teach the language arts as well as the content areas, such as social studies?

Regardless of the separate categories by which they are normally organized, the content areas and language arts are integrally related. Language in its four basic forms—reading, writing, listening, and speaking—is the means by which children obtain and convey information about **any** subject in the curriculum. On the other hand, the content areas provide the substance which serves to stimulate children's need to communicate. Moreover, thought processes central to learning, such as remembering, organizing, and evaluating information, cut across the entire curriculum. Organizing themes in children's literature and history, for example, call upon children to collect information, consider its worth, and then arrange that information into some kind of logical form. Additionally, cogent research has made it increasingly evident that children learn communication skills not by the artificial practice found in most language textbooks, but by engaging in real "languaging" activities that allow them to listen, speak, read, and write in natural and meaningful contexts (Halliday, 1982).

The content areas are abundantly rich with ideas and concepts that can come to life through the use of a variety of language arts activities. Accordingly, there is growing insight into the premise that substantive and varied language activities used for content area instruction actually serve to clarify and strengthen children's understanding of the subject matter (Tovey and Weible, 1981, 1979; Dolgin, 1981). And as children hear, talk, read and write about topics in that content area through the integrating vehicle of a unit, they become thoroughly involved in making sense of the material, relating it to what they already know, and formulating some brand new ideas of their own. It is highly likely that careful integration of the two spheres will result in mutual reinforcement and increased facility in **both** areas, as well as creating children who are sensitive to each other and eager learners.

Goals of an Integrated Unit

"Unit teaching" simply means that the chosen subject matter is organized into one complete whole, rather than taught as a series of isolated subjects. The body of knowledge to be conveyed to children is related, integrated, and correlated with memorable experiences so that the intellectual, social, emotional, and physical needs of children can be met on an individual basis (Smith, 1979). Through unit use, the teacher can develop group concepts without sacrificing the individual development of each child. The bottom line is that unit teaching can be viewed as a cross-curricular method of teaching that has the best chance of developing both the understanding of concepts and the creative intrapersonal communication skills that are needed in an Affective Language Arts program.

An effective integrated teaching unit should have these distinguishing characteristics:

1) It has a central, dominating theme;
2) It is based on the needs of a particular group of children;
3) It is planned cooperatively with that group of children;
4) It cuts across subject lines;
5) It provides a wide range of experiences so that children can grasp the concepts according to their own level of maturity;
6) It develops critical thinking skills;
7) It guides children toward creative thinking and self-realization;
8) It provides open-ended experiences which allow children to problem-solve;
9) It fosters good human relationships among children;
10) It requires a large block of time.

Planning an Integrated Unit

Often a unit of study is launched when a question is raised by the children in a particular classroom. The question might address some practical problem of society that could be adjusted for study at the elementary school level. Such a problem might be local, such as "What can we do to increase the ecological awareness of the people of Greenville so that Bond Lake might again be clean enough for swimming?" Or the question could be more global in nature, such as, "How did the problems that Blacks encountered before the Civil Rights Movement of the '50s compare with the Apartheid Policy in South Africa today?" These kinds of questions require in-depth exploration and discussion in order to develop the understandings necessary to really answer the questions; children must obtain a great deal of information, but it goes much deeper than that. Children will also need to become aware of the feelings and attitudes of people, discover how values, appreciations and character are developed in people and learn how to empathize with them so that the question can be seen and felt from a variety of viewpoints. The process of answering the question, then, becomes more important than the "solution" itself. For it is in the process of exploration that a unit provides that children come face to face with situations that force them to develop sensitivity to others while learning how to make their own decisions. In short, by using a unit approach to answer children's self-initiated questions, they learn about themselves and how to live with other human beings.

When beginning a unit, the major task of the teacher is to stimulate all the children in the class to be invested intellectually, socially, emotionally, and physically in the topic to be studied. Superficially, the interest would seem to be already there, as the original question has emanated from the group as a whole. But a deeper motivation stems from the act of establishing a sense of group mission that will ensure cooperative effort on the part of the teacher and students over a protracted period of time. Involving ALL the children is of vital concern and is best addressed by thoughtfully planning a large variety of ways for children to set about exploring the question so that each child can learn in the manner that he or she learns best.

To plan a unit which has the greatest chance of deeply involving all children in the exploration of the question, the teacher must be well prepared. First of all, she needs to be thoroughly versed in the subject matter, or the unit will certainly lack direction, focus and cohesion if she "learns as she goes." Secondly, she needs to outline the unit and gather relevant materials by following a guideline such as the one provided by these nine questions:

1.   Why did you select this particular unit?
   - Did it spring from questions the children have asked?
   - Are you interested in it?
   - Is the topic timely?

- Are materials available for use by or with the children?

2. What are the global cognitive and affective objectives you have in mind as important in developing through the unit?
   - What are your long-range objectives?
   - What are the children's objectives?
   - What are the outcomes you anticipate?

3. What are some motivational ways you can introduce the unit that will enlist the commitment of ALL learners?

4. What are the principles, understandings, or general information you want the children to come away with?

5. What activities and/or experiences can you plan that will span the entire curriculum and arouse the interest of each learner?
   - What community resources (e.g., guest speakers) are available?
   - What trade books can be gathered on the topic?
   - What research can be correlated with the topic?
   - What field trips could be planned?
   - What creative experiences could enhance the topic? (Drawings, paintings, murals, recipes, poems, plays, songs, folk tales, dances, etc.)
   - What other language experiences could be planned? (Debates, buzz groups, mock game shows, panel discussions, choral readings, discussion groups, etc.)

6. What culminating activity can you plan that will provide closure to the whole unit? (Dramatic production, assembly program, parents' night, feast, party, excursion, etc.)

7. What materials can you use as resources? (Community members, learning centers, bulletin boards, filmstrips, videos, movies, textbooks, etc.)

8. What materials can be provided for the children? (Trade books on different levels, commercial games,

songs, teacher-made games, computer simulations, etc.)
9.   How will you evaluate the effectiveness of the unit?
   ● Criterion tests (pre- and post)?
   ● Attitude scales?
   ● Daily observation?
   ● Individual conferences?
   ● Anecdotal records?
   ● Essays requiring analysis?
   ● Creative work springing from the topic?

Constructing a Curriculum Web

When all of the above questions have been considered, the teacher will be ready to organize the materials and activities for the duration of the unit. A graphic way to do this is through the use of a device known as the curriculum web (Moore et al., 1986). This framework helps the teacher to think of many possible ideas for the unit and then provides a visual structure which aids in the daily planning of the unit. To construct such a web, the teacher simply writes the question that the children have asked in the center of a large sheet of poster paper or tag board. Then he lets obvious subtopics branch off from the question by brainstorming available materials and activities that could be included to span all areas of the curriculum for each subtopic. For example, on the following page is an example of a sketch of a curriculum web for the question, "How are modern times rooted in the Middle Ages?"

Teaching an Integrated Unit

If a teacher were to decide to explore the unit based upon the curriculum web just presented, his objectives might be to acquaint children with the people, institutions, customs, and events of that thousand year period, and to help children to recognize, through this encounter, that some aspects of modern society have their roots in ideas and events of the Middle Ages. experiences

**Social Life
Activities**
Diorama of medieval life
Reenact a joust
Construct a medieval castle
Display of medieval garb
Crafts popular during the era
Medieval feast

Books
Knights of Old
Folk Tales of the Middle Ages
Anne: Child of the Middle Ages
Life in a Castle

Culture Activities
Tell stories of knights
    going to battle
Research medieval religions
Perform a medieval skit
Lecture by members of
    historical society
Sing ballads from the
    Middle Ages
Perform folk dances of the era
Make individual Coats-of-Arms

Books
Culture of the Middle Ages
Growing Up in the Dark Ages
Medieval Ballads

HOW ARE MODERN TIMES ROOTED IN THE MIDDLE AGES?

Political Issues Activities
Maps of ancient boundaries
Design a feudal pyramid
Computer simulation: Feudalism

Books
The Feudal System
The Dark Ages: A Political
    Perspective
The Feudal Pyramid

Language Activities
Research history of languages
Trace language to roots
Explore worlds of Middle Ages

Books
Tracing Our Language
Language in the Middle Ages
A Brief History of Languages

A variety of multimedia activities and cross-curricular experiences could be included to capture children's attention, to stimulate their thinking, and of course, to promote development in reading, writing, speaking, and listening skills.

From the start, children would be actively involved in discussing the proposed course of study. A teacher-written overview of concepts, vocabulary, and instructional goals might provide a springboard for reflection and a sharing of more new questions. Children would be encouraged to think about what facets of the unit might especially appeal to them, to share any prior knowledge about the topic, and to speculate on the importance of the unit to their own lives.

The dominant vehicle for unifying the content area of social studies with the language arts might, in this case, consist of a newspaper project in which children must report with as much historical accuracy as possible, life as it was in the Middle Ages. Although children would be well aware that newspapers were nonexistent in the Middle Ages, they could still use that well-known medium to convey their knowledge about the era to others. This extended project would involve children in a variety of language-centered activities, from seeking and gathering information to evaluating the importance of that information. Although the medieval newspaper would be the focal point of the unit, a number of other activities could be closely linked to it. These activities might include lectures on medieval life by costume-garbed members of a local historical society and demonstrations of arts and crafts that were popular during the era. Throughout the unit, classroom interactions would be varied, allowing children to work individually as well as in small and large groups.

Children's work would be evaluated continuously. Sometimes the evaluation might take the form of direct oral feedback to a child on work-in-progress via an informal conference. At other times, the evaluation could be offered as written comments or a grade on completed, formally submitted tasks.

Students' listening skills would be tapped by videos, filmstrips and books read to them about medieval life. Children would discuss social happenings of the nobility, the clergy and peasants, and simulate these events through computer programs. They would also talk about the economic and political issues of the time. These discussions, supplemented by films, computer programs, stories, and skits, would take on added importance because children would be aware that the knowledge gleaned would soon be transmitted to others through their newspaper articles and illustrations.

Throughout the unit, the most valuable sources for developing communication proficiency would undoubtedly be the children themselves as they interact with each other and the teacher. Effective listening and speaking are most critical when children are engaging in the hands-on projects that could be offered: the construction of a small-scale medieval castle, the creation of a personal coat of arms, and the assembling of several displays of medieval tools, clothing, personages, and scenes.

As children progressively gather more information and increase their understanding of the unit's concepts, they would be asked to share this new knowledge through formally and informally structured presentations; for example, groups of children might take turns role-playing different medieval scenarios. During these language activities children would be dramatically increasing their communication skills while literally immersing themselves in medieval life and tradition.

Children's awareness and appreciation of cultural and linguistic differences could be heightened with this unit by tracing the Spanish and English languages back to their Romance and Germanic roots. Children would also be exploring the different functions of all languages by using language for a number of different purposes: as they describe and reenact a sports event, such as jousting; as they invent and tell stories laced with imaginary episodes of knights going into battle; or as they recount and explain the symbolic information in their coats-of-arms.

By using the language arts in this wide variety of ways, children would be exercising their burgeoning understanding of concepts while stretching their intrapersonal communication abilities as well.

One added bonus to the unit approach is that, because of its interdisciplinary nature, the teacher need not worry that one isolated subject is "suffering" when the class is concentrating so intensely on the concepts of another isolated subject. Therefore, any unit need not be terminated until: 1) all the resources for the unit have been depleted, or 2) children's questions have been answered to their satisfaction and the teacher's objectives have been met, or 3) the interest of the class has waned, which may well never happen!

Literature-Based Units

An equally valid way to approach an integrated unit of study is through literature. Using this approach, instead of content area material being taught through the language arts, children's literature is the focus and is enhanced by spilling its message over into all crannies of the curriculum. Every goal of an Affective Language Arts program can be accomplished using children's literature in this way: listening improves as children listen purposefully, with rapt attention, to stories they grow to love; speaking improves as they eagerly discuss their reactions to the story. Many pieces of children's literature are excellent models for children's writing, and they can inspire students to try their hands at creating their own stories. And, of course, because they are not fraught with the idea of tedious skill development and stilted, controlled vocabulary, children's books are those that can most easily motivate children to read—for their own enjoyment.

Not only does children's literature provide a holistic framework for the development of listening, speaking, writing, and reading, but it can also be the cornerstone of a unit that provides stimulating lessons in all the other areas of the curriculum. This can be seen in the example of a unit centered around the book for primary-aged youngsters, *The Gingerbread Boy.*

Math
Make gingerbread cookies
   following a recipe and
   measuring ingredients.
Discuss ordinal numbers
   that could be used in
   the story: first he ran
   from the bird, second
   from the rabbit, etc.

Art
Paint a sequential mural
   of events in the story.
Make papier-mache masks of
   characters in the story
   for use in retelling.
Make a diorama of a favorite
   scene from the story.

THE GINGERBREAD BOY

Language Arts
Have children tape their
   version of the story.
Compare the story with
   The Bun (Brown).
Create a skit of the story.

Science/Health
Research what all animals
   in the story really eat.
Discuss how gingerbread
   cookies can fit into
   a balanced diet.

Music
Make up a song about
   the Gingerbread Boy.
Listen to "Peter and the
   Wolf" while doing other
   activities.
Discuss what instruments
   could be used for animals
   in "The Gingerbread Boy."

Social Studies
Make a topographical map of
   the Gingerbread Boy's
   journey.
Discuss the natural enemies
   of all the animals in
   the story.
Discuss the cookie's behavior
   toward his parents.

Summary

The teaching unit has been around for many years, but has traditionally been thought of as the exclusive domain of the social sciences. In light of what we now know to be true of the need to integrate the language arts into meaningful contexts, the unit would seem the natural vehicle through which this integration could best flourish. With careful planning on the part of the teacher, the very important questions that children ask can become dominating themes for language-centered units that cross every boundary of the curriculum, providing stimulating experiences that totally immerse children in the process of answering their own questions. And through this special process, children learn to empathize with another's point of view and crystallize their **own** viewpoints at the same time. They learn to work cooperatively in small groups, large groups, and by themselves under the teacher's watchful guidance. The variety of activities offered allows all children, regardless of their ability, to understand at some level the major concepts of the unit, according to their own styles of learning.

This integration of the curriculum can also spring from the exciting world of children's books. Any one of a number of excellent selections from children's literature could be expanded to include tangential lessons spanning the entire curriculum, while enhancing and deepening children's understanding of and appreciation for those books.

The integrated unit—whether germinating from a child's question or from children's literature—has one overriding characteristic that would earn it a place of honor in an Affective Language Arts program: this unique approach makes the learner a vitally active participant in the learning process. For too many years educators have labored under the arrogant assumption that students must learn solely from their teachers. It takes only one well-planned unit to graphically illustrate to all who care to observe that yes, children do learn from the teacher, but they can also learn many, many important things by themselves and from each other.

References

Brown, M. *The Bun*. New York: Harcourt Brace Jovanovich, 1972.

Dolgin, A.B. "Teaching Social Studies through Writing." *Social Studies* 72 (January-February 1981): pp. 8-10.

Halliday, M.A.K. "Three Aspects of Children's Language Development: Learning Language, Learning through Language, and Learning about Language." Y. Goodman, M. Hausler and D. Strickland (eds.). *Oral and Written Language Development Research: Impact on the Schools*. National Council of Teachers of English, 1982.

Holdsworth, W.C. *The Gingerbread Boy*. New York: Farrar, Straus, & Giroux, 1968.

Moore, D.W., S.A. Moore, P.M. Cunningham, and J.W. Cunningham. *Developing Readers and Writers in the Content Areas*. New York: Longman, 1986.

Smith, F. *Writing and the Writer*. New York: Holt, Rinehart and Winston, 1982.

Smith, J.A. *Creative Teaching of the Social Studies in the Elementary School*. Boston: Allyn and Bacon, 1979.

Tovey, D.R. and T.D. Weible. "Social Studies, Thought, and Language." *Social Studies* 70 (July-August 1979): pp. 167-69.

_____. "Extending Social Studies Understanding through Language Activities." *Social Education* 45 (May 1981): pp. 367-69.

Yopp, R.H. and H.K. Yopp. *Literature-Based Reading Activities*. Boston: Allyn and Bacon, 1992.

Chapter Twelve

Learning Stations:
Child-Centered Language Learning

Mr. Trainor has just been assigned his very first class—a fourth grade—and he surveys his eager charges with mounting dismay. He finds that within his class are Jesús, age seven; Michael, age eight; Dorothy, age nine; Debra, age ten; and Martha, age eleven. There is one other seven-year-old like Jesus, a half dozen eight-year-olds, like Michael, and almost a dozen nine-year-olds like Dorothy, as well as a couple more eleven-year-olds, like Martha. The ages of Mr. Trainor's students just mentioned are not their chronological ages, but their mental ages, or the ages at which they are currently functioning intellectually. This intellectual spread is not at all unusual in a fourth grade classroom, and the differences of the children do not stop there. Mr. Trainor also finds that his students vary widely in the styles in which they learn best, and the pace at which they can assimilate concepts. He also notices an enormous discrepancy in the kinds of activities and reading materials that appeal to the children of this class, as well as their command, in some cases, of English as a second language.

But poor Mr. Trainor's curriculum is all planned for his fourth-graders; his textbooks were purchased with the "average" nine-year-old in mind, and he is duly expected to get all the children ready for fifth grade by the end of the year. This is the dilemma of teachers everywhere; Mr. Trainor's class is no exception. And as long as we ignore the realities and act as though the differences do not exist, we will ALWAYS continue to struggle with the dilemma, and neither carte blanche promotion nor a return to systematically retaining "underachievers" will make it go away.

161

The development and use of learning stations is one effective method of achieving some measure of individualization of instruction. It is not intended as a panacea to all classroom problems and it will certainly not satisfy all the needs of all the learners in a classroom. But it can be an effective approach for moving children away from rigidly uniform whole-group learning experiences targeted to the "average" child in a classroom, and toward student-selected, individual and small group learning experiences.

The learning station is not meant to replace the teacher and his humanizing influence in the classroom, nor can a station be expected to be the prime source of instruction in the classroom. It can, however, be used in an Affective Language Arts program to provide the necessary reinforcement for expansion on, and enrichment of, those concepts and skills which have previously been introduced by the teacher. Moreover, a well-planned learning center is often so attractive and inviting that even the most reluctant learner is easily lured to it. Children, before the teacher's very eyes, become intensely involved in exploring a wide variety of interesting topics in the way that youngsters feel the most comfortable—by actively experiencing them, at their own pace, through their senses.

Pre-Planning for a Learning Station

In developing educationally sound, stimulating learning stations which have the best chance of meeting the needs of the children in a particular class, the secret is pre-planning. Each center should be carefully planned with specific objectives in mind for the need of the range of learners in the class. Each center must not only meet the needs of the average and slow learners, but challenge the intellectually talented as well.

The following criteria are helpful to consider when first attempting to construct learning stations (Smith, 1979):

1)   **A learning station should have specific objectives.** A survey of student needs through pre-testing may be the teacher's best guide to the type of center to be developed. First, the

teacher must determine the center's major objective. Second, the teacher must decide upon a variety of activities which will help children to realize that goal. Finally, the teacher needs to plan a method of evaluating whether or not the children have met the objective. For example, the purpose of one learning station might be to familiarize children with folk tales from other countries. The teacher's specific objective might be stated like this: "As a result of the activities in this learning station, the children will be able to write a new folk tale based upon the fictitious customs of a country which the child has created."

2)   **The theme of the learning station should lend itself to integration across the curriculum.** Literacy in and of itself has no discrete content; the station's theme could be culled from social studies or science and contain reading, writing, listening and speaking experiences as well as art, math, etc. (Crawford, 1993).

3)   **A learning station must be well equipped.** In order to present a broad scope of multisensory activities which will best accommodate the range of learning styles in a classroom, a wide variety of materials must be gathered. For instance, a folk tale center would need a globe, maps of the various countries represented, trade books of folk tales from other lands, filmstrips, a tape recorder for the oral telling of stories, puppets and a puppet theater in which to perform folk tales, shoe boxes for dioramas, writing paper and utensils, encyclopedias, a dictionary, a file of duplicating masters, and a costume box with costumes to inspire skits, and packets for individual contracts.

4)   **A learning station should be colorful and attractive.** Whether the intent of the learning station is skills development, enrichment, or sheer fun (or, ideally, a combination of all three), inviting packaging will enhance the appeal and greatly increase children's motivation to spend time there. The overall impression children should have as they approach the station is one of very high visual attractiveness, cohesion and harmony. Even if "beauty is only skin deep," the look of the station should grab children's attention and make them eager to explore its contents.

5)   **A learning station must be functional.** A functional station is well aligned with the purposes of the Affective Language Arts program. This means that the station must be well-planned in keeping with the station objectives, inviting enough to attract children, and equipped with enough language activities and equipment so that all children may independently learn from working in it without direct teacher supervision. There must also be provisions for small groups of children to work together cooperatively.

6)   **The activities in a learning station must facilitate self-learning.** Once the overall instructions and objectives for the learning station have been explained by the teacher to the entire class, children should be able to be in charge of their own learning by means of contracts between the teacher and student, records kept by the teacher and student, and evaluations in which children play an active role. Additionally, many activities may be designed so that they are programmed or involve self-checking, so that children can begin to monitor their own progress.

7)   **The activities in the learning station should concern situations that are authentic.** Children should have an opportunity to use reading, writing, listening, and speaking in ways that are as close to real-world settings as possible (Crawford, 1993).

Arranging a Learning Station

The best room arrangement technique, particularly when a teacher is planning to use more than one learning station at a time, is to make small clusters, or "learning pockets" around the periphery of the room, but there is really no right or wrong way to arrange a learning station. The teacher must simply use his imagination and resources to make the center physically fit the needs of his students within the constraints of his own classroom.

The flat-topped, individual desks or large four- to eight-student tables with separate chairs are the most convenient to use for learning stations, but slanting desks can be used for individual study centers or individual activities. Also, slanting desks can be effectively used as writing surfaces when the stations are located on shelves or walls. Games could be played on an old shag rug on the floor. Other pieces of furniture that can assist in organizing the station would be bookcases, dividers, book racks, and painting easels. Overstuffed chairs, a couch, or bean bag chairs will also add to the physical appeal of a station and might be used for a reading or library corner. Bulletin boards should be an integral part of a station, and bright contact paper and paint could be used to liven up drab pieces of furniture. Children are usually happy to assist in these refurbishing chores and such tasks add to their sense of ownership of the learning station.

Scheduling for Learning Stations

The amount of time to be scheduled at learning stations depends upon what kinds of activities are contained in the station and how the activities have been integrated across the curriculum. Obviously, there is no right or wrong scheduling plan as long as the teacher feels comfortable with the time spent in the station, the children are actively engaged in learning through station activities, and the needs of the entire range of students are being met.

Schedules provide children with an outline for using their time beneficially. Moreover, the children develop a sense of security as well as a sense of responsibility by keeping track of what they will be doing daily at the station. There are two basic systems for scheduling students into stations, by rotation and by contract.

● **Rotational.** When multiple stations are being used in a classroom, rotational scheduling is a good introductory format because it allows the children to sample a bit of everything that is offered in the classroom. Using this scheduling format, stations are set up around the room and children can be managed by use of an "assignment wheel" such as this one:

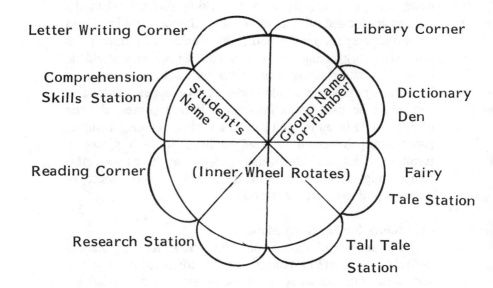

Letter Writing Corner

Library Corner

Comprehension
Skills Station

Student's
Name

Group Name
or number

Dictionary
Den

Reading Corner

(Inner Wheel Rotates)

Fairy
Tale Station

Research Station

Tall Tale
Station

● **Contracting.** A "contract" is a written agreement between student and teacher, and can be drawn up for each child after a new learning station has initially been introduced to a group of children. Each child decides exactly what he would like to accomplish in a station in order to meet the specific goals that the teacher has established for the station. Student-teacher conferences are arranged in which the child shares orally what he has agreed to do in his written contract. By this method, children learn to monitor their own work habits and use of time. Often children put too much in their contract and are then unable to complete the work by the date to which they have agreed. The teacher then needs to help the child to realistically determine a reasonable amount of work to be included on a contract.

A simple contract might be put onto a ditto master and made available within the learning station. Page 167 shows an example of a learning station contract.

CONTRACT FOR: _____

Date Started: _____

Activity	Comments	Activity	Comments

Date completed: _____

Teacher signature: _____

Student signature: _____

Comments: _____

_____

_____

_____

Record Keeping for Learning Stations

In order to properly evaluate each child's progress in a learning station, the teacher must keep adequate accounts of what each child is doing. This is a continuous process involving both the teacher and the child. Records show the kind and the amount of work a child accomplishes. An evaluation, on the other hand, reflects the quality of that work. The type of records that need to be kept will vary depending upon the areas covered by the learning station.

One common type of record keeping for a station is the student file of completed work. For this file, the teacher and child set priorities for work to be completed and then establish a schedule for daily, weekly, and monthly activities. To each file is attached a teacher comment sheet. Comments are written in the file every week so that children can modify their work habits. These comments also help to prepare the teacher for the student-teacher conferences.

A chart showing what each child has read is another record keeping device that is of supreme importance in a learning station. Because the information on this chart is a tangible reflection of accomplishment, it serves to satisfy the child's need for recognition of progress and achievement. It also encourages recreational reading in areas that may have been new to the child. The reading chart should be displayed in or near the learning station so that the children themselves become responsible for updating the record as more and more books are completed.

Records can also be kept for a station that is accentuating specific skill development. For this type of record keeping, the teacher needs to list the specific skill objectives on the student record sheet. Each station should have a sheet that lists all tasks, each one of which would be designed to reinforce a certain skill. Older children would be able to check off the tasks as they are completed. Younger children can color a square or have the teacher check off the task. An example of a record-evaluation sheet for a set of tasks in a learning station is on page 169.

Sample Evaluation of Student Work at Station

Marking System:
+ understands concept; assign to more challenging task
/ meeting objective; continue through task
- needs assistance; reteaching
Title of Activity: Dictionary Teasers
Objective: Using the dictionary, the student will be able to
sort sets of twelve words into the categories of
animals, plants, or inanimate objects.

Date	Name:	1	2	3	4*	5	6	7	8	9*	10
Comments:											

* Tasks that require teacher correction.
Suggestion: Use graph paper to make record sheets.

Holistic Evaluation in a Learning Station

Evaluation of a child's work at a learning station is much more than a letter grade at the completion of some self-selected station activities; it is an ongoing, continuous affair. Evaluations included on all record sheets in the form of comments and self-correcting materials give children immediate feedback for self-appraisal. During student-teacher conferences children offer and receive suggestions for improvement. "Spot checking," too, is an important evaluation tool as children are actively involved in independent learning. As the teacher makes observations, he writes anecdotal comments on the child's work folder immediately. Additionally, children may share projects orally with the whole class and relate their new discoveries and experiences, giving the teacher an even greater insight into what his students have assimilated.

But evaluation in an Affective Language Arts program means much more than just looking at children's cognitive accomplishments. The affective teacher is interested in the growth of the whole child: the rate, the process, the child's reactions and attitudes, his products, and any new behaviors that have developed in the child as a result of working in that station.

There are several kinds of positive attitudes and behaviors that ideally should evolve from a learning station experience:

● Children will have worked in groups, cooperatively and productively.

● Children will have grown in independent work habits.

● Children will have demonstrated increased ability to plan their time.

● Children will have discovered some creative new ways to work together and by themselves.

● Children will have explored some new areas of interest.

● Children will have participated in the evaluation of their own work.

Based upon these expectations, the evaluation form on the next page might help the teacher to look more thoroughly at how the "whole child" has benefited as a result of working at the learning station.

Summary

Learning stations work in an Affective Language Arts program because it is a truism that no two children are exactly alike, and the station allows the teacher to develop a variety of inviting activities and materials which actually cater to individual differences. The affective teacher in today's schools is sensitive to the vast differences in ability, learning styles, and interests of

Evaluation of Child's Learning Station Experience

Student:_____

Date:_____

Rating Scale
1 2 3 4 5   Comments
Low   High

A. How well does this child:
   1. Follow oral & written directions?
       1 2 3 4 5 _____
   2. Complete station tasks?
       1 2 3 4 5 _____
   3. Interact with other children in a helping or sharing
       situation?   1 2 3 4 5 _____
   4. Take responsibility for group learning?
       1 2 3 4 5 _____
   5. Use his/her time?
       1 2 3 4 5 _____
   6. Explore new areas of interest?
       1 2 3 4 5 _____
   7. Ask questions that go beyond the scope of the
       activity?   1 2 3 4 5 _____
   8. Communicate thoughts and ideas to classmates?
       1 2 3 4 5 _____
   9. Devise ways to use materials or make suggestions for
       the stations? 1 2 3 4 5 _____
   10. Complete plans made in student-teacher conferences?
       1 2 3 4 5 _____

Comments:_____

_____

her pupils; indeed, it is not uncommon for five or six grade levels of ability and achievement to be represented in a single classroom! This reality tends to make assignments targeted to the class as a whole a waste of time for many children. There is no longer any justifiable reason for every child in a class to always learn the same thing, in the same way, in the same amount of time, from the same material, with the same amount of interest. The learning station seems to be one viable solution to this dilemma.

Learning stations build stimulating group experiences into the learning process. The child is offered these group situations, but is also offered opportunities to work independently. By working together cooperatively, children learn how to respectfully exchange ideas and share the responsibility for learning.

If, in the development of an exciting and inviting learning station, the teacher is attentive to individual interests, learning styles, ability differences, and the range of English language proficiency in the class, the learning station will probably be a success. When in addition, each child is involved in setting goals, the selection of the learning activities and materials, the pace at which she will work, and the evaluation of that work, then success is virtually assured. These successful experiences will, in turn, enhance the self-concept of the child. Too, the chances are then excellent that the teacher will be forever "hooked" on the learning station approach to learning as an affective way to help meet the needs of all children.

References

Blitz, B. *The Open Classroom: Making It Work*. Boston: Allyn and Bacon, 1973.

Crawford, L.W. *Language and Literacy Learning in Multicultural Classrooms*. Boston: Allyn and Bacon, 1993.

Gagne, R. *The Conditions of Learning*. 3rd ed. New York: Holt, Rinehart & Winston, 1977.

Johnston, H., et al. *The Learning Center Ideabook*. Boston: Allyn and Bacon, 1978.

Musgrave, R.G. *Individualized Instruction: Teaching Strategies Focusing on the Learner*. Boston: Allyn and Bacon, 1975.

Petreshene, S.S. *Complete Guide to Learning Centers*. Palo Alto, CA: Pendragon House, 1978.

Rapport, V., ed. *Learning Centers: Children on Their Own*. Washington DC: Association for Childhood Education International, 1970.

Smith, J.A. *Creative Teaching of Social Studies in the Elementary School*. Boston: Allyn and Bacon, 1979.

Chapter Thirteen

Literacy and the Arts:
Voices for Diverse Learners

Ramón is molding his piece of clay into a monster that he just encountered while listening to his teacher read *Where the Wild Things Are* (Sendak, 1963). This pliable medium helps him to think about his reaction to the frightening text. Wa Meng conceptualizes what has occurred in the same story through the use of a pa ndau, or Hmong flower cloth, which is the traditional way of telling stories in his culture. Nicoli responds to a recording of *Flight of the Bumblebee* by breathlessly recounting the tale of losing control of his bicycle while going down a steep hill, while José shares a frenetic morning of getting ready to catch the school bus that the same piece of music brings to HIS mind.

The above children are demonstrating the infinite possibilities for integrating the arts into all areas of literacy development—and into the lives of every child. Music, oral interpretations, dance, discussions about art and photography were once thought of as enrichment activities, often reserved for only the highest functioning students, or utilized as occasional breaks from the teaching of the "fundamental" skills of reading, writing, listening, and speaking. All that is changing in the 90s. The classroom of the 90s is a vastly different place than that of even a decade ago, and the arts may be the very answer to many of the needs brought about by these changes.

Children in today's schools are widely diverse, coming from a variety of ethnic, linguistic, and cultural backgrounds. From this heterogeneous garden, children at all stages of literacy development can find expression for their thoughts, values, ideas, and feelings through the arts. Due to their backgrounds, certain children may understand and express concepts better through art than they ever could through the written word; some of these children may understand and express themselves better through one art form than another. For one child, music may speak with the greatest clarity; to another, a painting conveys the strongest message; to yet another dance possesses the most profound appeal. Regardless of the medium used to convey the concepts to learners, many individual underlying messages can come across.

An example of a cultural group for whom the arts are particularly relevant are the Hmong. Within the last few years approximately 100,000 Hmong families have found their way to our shores from refugee camps along the Thai-Laotian border. Unlike other groups, the Hmong have an exclusively oral tradition, with no written language as we commonly think of it. Instead, magnificently-detailed Hmong needlework represents their changing record of history; likewise, tribal traditions are conceptualized in elaborate jewelry. In fact, clothing designs seen recently being worn by the Hmong people, of red, white, and blue, as in the American flag, clearly show the Hmong people wish to assimilate and adopt a new culture (Livo & Cha, 1991).

The Hmong culture is a strong case for the arts in today's classrooms. How would teachers best reach Hmong youngsters who readily conceptualize ideas with art, but who initially may flounder when confronted with written language? Again—the arts, in their broadest sense, are the answer. While art can mean what is traditionally termed the "fine arts," it is also used, for the purpose of this chapter to include needlework, carpentry, jewelry-making, folktales through murals—or any other conceivable expression of the human spirit.

Diverse Voices for Diverse Learners

Since the days of the enlightenment, educators have been behaving as though there were only two ways of being intelligent—through verbal or mathematical abilities. The work of cognitive psychologist Howard Gardner (1990) suggests now that there are at least seven discrete kinds of intelligences to consider: linguistic, musical, logical-mathematical, spatial, bodily-kinesthetic, interpersonal, and intrapersonal, suggesting that there are at least five other pathways that we could be utilizing in schools to allow children to express what they know. Moreover, many children, non-native English speakers and English speakers alike, come to school with abundant knowledge and rich ideas, but they often differ from those of the dominant culture, or they are ideas that are hard to express through the traditional verbal and mathematical channels. To appreciate the richness and diversity in a particular classroom, teachers may wish to consider each of their students in relation to the checklist on the following pages.

The remainder of this chapter will offer suggestions as to how affective teachers can tap the often-neglected "other" intelligences of their learners through the use of drama, singing, music, art, photography, and dance.

Drama

Children with natural bodily-kinesthetic abilities often delight in showing what they know through drama and pantomime. Such activities foster positive interaction with peers and enhance interest in other forms of symbolic representation. Moreover, any acting out of ideas offers second-language learners a means of comprehensible input or what Faltis (1993) calls "nonverbal support" for the concepts which are being conveyed.

Skits can be created when children have read a story that they really liked, or when such a story has been read to them by the teacher. Afterward the teacher asks the children to discuss their favorite scenes from the story. Usually, the children will tend to choose scenes that are the most appropriate for dramatization (this isn't as unlikely as it seems; children are drawn to scenes with the most intensity, whether it is sad, funny, exciting, or scary).

LEARNING DIFFERENCES QUESTIONNAIRE (STUDENT)

Student's Name: _____

Does this student:

1. Linguistic
___like to write stories?

___spin tall tales or tell jokes and stories?

___have a good memory for names, places, dates and trivia?

___play and win at word games (scrabble, anagrams, etc.)?

___enjoy reading books in his/her spare time?

___spell words accurately and easily?

___appreciate nonsense rhymes, tongue-twisters, etc.?

2. Logical-Mathematical
___ask a lot of questions about how things work?

___compute arithmetic problems in his/her head quickly?

___enjoy math class?

___find computer programs interesting?

___play chess, checkers or other strategy games and win?

___spend hours working on logic puzzles like Rubik's cube?

___enjoy putting things in categories and hierarchies?

3. Spatial
___report clear visual images when thinking about something?

___read maps, charts and diagrams easily?

___daydream a lot during class?

___enjoy art activities?

___draw accurate representations of people or things?

___like it when you have movies or slides in class?

___enjoy doing jigsaw puzzles or mazes?

4. Bodily-Kinesthetic
___excel in competitive sports?

___move, twitch, tap or fidget while sitting at a desk?

___cleverly mimic other people's gestures or mannerisms?

___love to take things apart and put them back together again?

___put his/her hands all over something he/she's just seen?

___spend recess running, jumping, wrestling, etc.?

___demonstrate skill in a craft (e.g., woodworking, mechanics)?

5. Musical

___tell you when a musical note is off-key?

___remember melodies of songs?

___sing on key?

___listen to songs on the radio or stereo every day?

___claims he/she needs to have music on in order to study?

___has lots of records or tapes at home?

___remember TV jingles or theme songs?

6. Interpersonal

___hang around after school and socialize?

___seem to be a natural leader?

___counsel friends who have problems?

___seem to be street-smart?

___hold class offices or head any clubs or committees?

___enjoy teaching other students?

___like playing card games, board games or other cooperative classroom activities?

7. Intrapersonal

___display a sense of independence or a strong will?

___react with strong opinions to controversy?

___do well when left alone to study?

___march to the beat of a different drummer?

___have an interest or hobby he/she doesn't talk much about?

___have "hunches" about things that turn out to be true?

___have a good sense of his/her own mood and behaviors?

As scenes from the story are being recalled by children, other class members can be encouraged to add important details in their own words. When children have finished recounting the scenes, the teacher can ask thought-provoking questions designed to have children think more deeply about the feelings and motivations of each character.

Questions such as the following, for example, would help children to think about the motivation of some of the characters: "How do you think Betsy felt when her father said she would have to find a new home for the kitten?" "What was her little brother's reaction?" "Did the mother seem to agree with the father's decision?" "How do you know?" "How did she show what she was feeling?"

When the children have finished retelling all the events in the story and have discussed the personalities and feelings of all the characters, they are ready to work on characterization. An effective technique to begin this phase, and one that allows second-language learners to really tune in to the story, is through pantomime. The children take turns acting out, with exaggerated actions and facial gestures, any of the characters in the story while the rest of the class tries to guess which character is being impersonated. As children guess, they join in the pantomime. Children should be encouraged to think about the character's mood, personality, whether (s)he is young or old, bold or shy, mean or kind, and how such attributes might affect the character's gait, expression, gestures, and general demeanor. If children have trouble developing a certain character's identity, an impromptu exercise can sometimes help. For example, if the children are having problems portraying José's dread as he approaches the haunted house, the teacher might instruct the class: "Imagine it is Halloween. It is a dark, windy, stormy night. You are going to knock on the door of an old mansion on the hill that everyone says is haunted. You can hear your heart beating in your chest; you are so frightened. Show how you approach the mansion. How would your voice sound? How would you move?"

After bringing the characters to life, the children are ready to act out the entire scene. Although some children may be reticent initially, the first volunteers will be having so much fun that others will be eager to join in. The teacher can facilitate most effectively by sitting on the sidelines and allowing children to cooperatively problem solve how each segment should be dramatized with occasional prompts, such as, "Isn't it time for Miss Luce to come along wondering where her kitten has gone?" It is also helpful for the teacher to ask the rest of the class not to interrupt a scene with suggestions; the children performing at any one time should have ownership of their ideas and be allowed to finish expressing them.

When the scene seems to be winding down the teacher can show appreciation of the performance by standing up, applauding, and giving very specific feedback to the actors: "I really enjoyed the way you showed you were old, Grandma, by stooping over and making your voice all quivery." At this juncture, the audience will be ready to try the same scene their way, having had an opportunity to reflect upon how they would alter the acting out of a certain character. The scene can then be repeated until all who wish to have had an opportunity to share their interpretation of a scene.

When several scenes have been "blocked" in this manner, children may wish to select songs that they have learned that the characters might sing, to add to the production. They may wish to add spontaneous dance movements to better emphasize the mood of certain characters. Finally, they can be encouraged to make their own background and props to add a visual element that enhances the audience's understanding of the setting.

Studio Art and Children's Literature

The spatial intelligence of children can be highlighted when children express themselves through art activities in response to children's literature they have read. Such integration, however, must be more than following the reading of a story about spring with an assignment that asks children to color flowers on a prepared ditto. Studio art and children's literature must be connected in such a way that children take away not only a deeper understanding of the story, through the art activity, but also a better appreciation of themselves as artists. One way to make this connection is by introducing children to children's literature that has main characters who are themselves artists and who share their feelings about themselves as artists. After reading such stories, children are inspired to try their hand at creating art in the same way that the main character has discussed in the book. For example, in the book *All I See*, by Cynthia Rylant, a little boy, Charlie, loves to paint. Every morning he goes down to the edge of a lake and hides as he watches Gregory, an artist, paint pictures of blue whales on his easel. When Gregory leaves, Charlie sneaks over to see what Gregory has painted that day. It is always the same—blue whales. One day when Charlie inspects the canvas it is blank, so he paints his own picture of Gregory painting and humming. The following day, when Charlie pads down to the lake to see what Gregory has painted, he sees only a sign, "I liked your picture." Later, Charlie and Gregory become friends and Gregory teaches Charlie about "...shadow and light, about line, about drawing things near and things far away..." (p. 21). Finally, Charlie musters the courage to ask Gregory the one thing he doesn't understand about the man's painting: why does he always paint pictures of blue whales when there are none in the lake? Gregory replies, "It is all I see." Charlie learns an important lesson about what "seeing" means to an artist.

Such a sensitive story can be used to underscore a very important concept about the nature of art: what one "sees" is not always with one's eyes. Many artists do NOT paint what is in their immediate environment, meticulously rendered, but rather what is in their heart.

Using visualization, children can be encouraged to use their own "mind's eye" to see in the way an artist might. The teacher can facilitate by taking children on a pretend "walking tour" through their homes, inviting children to evoke feeling, memories, aromas, textures of furniture, colors, brightness, mood, etc. Then, providing colored pencils, crayons, colored chalk, or paint, children may be invited to pictorialize their impressions, attempting to convey as much of their feelings as possible, just as Gregory did.

In a follow-up session, children are usually ready to move from the familiar to the unfamiliar with their artistic impressions. Using verbal cues similar to those offered in the previous activity, the teacher can guide the children to the edge of the very lake by which Charlie and Gregory painted. Providing painting materials, the teacher can encourage children to "paint all they see." The activity brings children to new levels of aesthetic sensitivity and offers a high regard for all children's own visions as artists.

Music and Singing

The musical intelligence of children can be highlighted in the classroom through a language arts program that includes a study of classical music and composers, singing, and music response journals.

Children can be systematically introduced to quality music over the nine months of the school year by having the teacher select several selections to be highlighted each month, generally related to the season or a holiday which takes place during that time. For example, April's selections might include Copland's *Appalachian Spring Suite* and Stravinsky's *Rites of Spring*. Each month as the new selections are introduced, the teacher discusses the composer and where he is from, what that country's language is, what the people eat, etc. with the help of a globe and pictures from an encyclopedia or other resources. The teacher also helps children understand how authors and composers are the same and different as they grow familiar with tunes just as they have become familiar with stories.

Monthly selections can be played during free reading time, as children are writing, as well as when the children first come in during the morning. Finally, as children have become familiar with each piece of music, the teacher may have children close their eyes and listen to the music for a specific instrument. After listening they can be invited to explain how they recognized that instrument. Why do they feel the composer chose that instrument?

Even mathematics can be brought into the arts and literacy programs as children are asked to respond to questions such as: "Which instruments did you like the best?" "Which instrument would **you** like to learn to play?" Children can then count the number of responses and the children, or the teacher for younger children, can graph the results.

Singing
   Singing can also be brought into a classroom to raise the status of children who have musical intelligence, although a "gift" for singing is not a necessary prerequisite for engaging in such a natural activity. All children can become joyful singers of songs.
   The following ideas will help teachers bring singing into the classroom in such a way that literacy will be enhanced:
   • Select a song that is a favorite of children, particularly one with simple words that contains plenty of rhyme, rhythm, and repetition. Invite children who speak languages other than English to teach the class songs in their language.
   • Write the lyrics of the chosen song on a large song chart. Have the group sing the song one phrase at a time. Model strategies for sounding out words by thinking aloud as the lyrics are written down.
   • Using a pointer, match each syllable with a note to stress the rhythm as the song is sung chorally.
   • When children are familiar with the tune, brainstorm new lyrics to the song, using the familiar tune. For example, when the children can sing "This Old Man," they will be ready to improvise new lyrics—in English and other languages—using the tune, meter, and repetition scheme provided by the original song.
   • Later children can learn that the notes of the scale have names; that the rhythm of the music depends on the number of beats in a measure, and that a written note of melody has both pitch and may be held for varying amounts of time. The similarities between written music and written words symbol systems can be pointed out. Just as authors write words for readers, composers write notes on a staff for singers to sing and musicians to play on their instruments.

Music Response Journals

Another way music can be brought into the classroom is via music response journals. To develop a deeper appreciation of so-called "quality" music, it is helpful to begin having children listen intently to music they already know and love—whether it is salsa, rap, folk, or rock n' roll. Ask children to bring in their favorite songs and set aside a few minutes each day to listen carefully to each song. To connect the two symbol systems, have children (or the teacher) transcribe the lyrics on a handout or the overhead projector so that children may follow along.

As children listen to each song, ask them to pay very close attention to the music, the words, the instruments that have been selected, the rhythm, and the mood that is created by the combination of these factors. As they are listening invite them to write down in their journals any thoughts, feelings, ideas, images, colors, impressions, or comments that come to their minds. Encourage those who are not fluent in written English to respond in their own language or through picture. The resultant stream of consciousness is often remarkable as children respond to the revisitation of "their" music with increased concentration.

Because the teacher has been open to the children's favorite music, they will find that the children are much more open to exploring unfamiliar music in the same manner. At this point, the teacher may want to choose classical music with much dramatic intensity, such as Grieg's "Hall of the Mountain King" or Rimsky-Korsakov's "Flight of the Bumblebee." As they listen intently to the music, ask them to "...imagine that your body has thousands and thousands of tiny pinpricks in it, so small that you can't even see them. Listen to the music and imagine that it must go through all those pinpricks before it can get inside of you. Once it gets through, it flows into all parts of you and fills you" (Chenfield, 1987). When children understand this metaphor, play the selected music for them. Afterward, invite them to record their auditory images—the feelings, colors, words, and memories they "saw," just as they did with the contemporary music.

Finally, encourage children to share their individual responses in small share groups.

Photography

In a photographic project, children have a unique opportunity to demonstrate an innate inter- and intrapersonal intelligence as they work cooperatively to compose photographs, problem solve issues of light, distance and composition, and self-assess their products.

The selection of a photographic project must reflect the interest of the student or students involved and thus result in active participation, planning, executing, evaluating and learning. A group of enthusiastic photographers might choose from any of the following possibilities:

a documentary on a particular subject

an autobiography

photos to accompany original poetry

a wordless picture book

a photographic essay

a photographic collage

a reflective journal with photographs

an advertising campaign

Besides the planning of the above activities, photography offers other chances for authentic literacy experiences as children must read directions for the use of cameras, maintain log books of equipment use, collaborate with peers, and articulate their reasons for liking or disliking certain photographs.

An exhibit gives photographers a chance to share their creations with a real audience. Such an activity would involve having children select their favorite photographs from their personal portfolios, mounting them attractively, arranging them in aesthetically pleasing ways, entitling the photographs, and creating announcements of the time and place for the photographic display. The selection process alone would provide new interpersonal insights.

Dance

Finally, there is perhaps no better way to highlight the talents of learners who possess bodily-kinesthetic abilities than by incorporating dance with literacy instruction. Dance also has a distinctly communicative nature; there are times when feelings, emotions, and ideas can best be expressed through body movements. Nonverbal body movements, as compared with other types of motor activities, can become voices for conceptualization, personal messages, and conveyors of cultural traditions and ideas. The ability to symbolize through dance, as in language, extends a child's knowledge of the world and its ways.

Literacy and dance can be integrated in an affective classroom after a variety of activities have allowed children to find their own personal significance in pieces of literature. Children read a book to themselves or with reading buddies, they form self-selected literature response groups, and then small groups of children choose to retell the story orally or to reenact it in skit form. They may also express their reactions to the literature in their literature response journals, excerpts of which they may select to share in their small groups.

After the children have had time to respond to the literature in these ways, the teacher sets aside time once or twice a week for the "dance workshop." During this time, children select one or two key ideas from the story to express in dance form. Specifically, they are asked to consider three elements of the story that lend themselves to body movement: mood, structure, and symbols, or extended metaphors (Eeds, 1990). The "structure" is the high point, or "climax" of the story and the author must build up to and then relieve, this tension. Children must decide what they think is the most intense point of the story and then decide how they would move their bodies to express this tension. The "mood" concerns the emotional state of the story, or perhaps the author's emotional state when the story was written. The children must use their bodies to express a happy, morose, scary, etc. mood. Finally, the "symbols," or "extended metaphor," concerns the "truth" of the story that is examined in an original way by the author. What have the children learned about life by reading this book? How can their bodies express this new knowledge?

When the children have created their own sequence of movements that symbolize their responses to key ideas in the book, they choose a piece of classical music to accompany their dance from the repertoire of pieces that have been introduced throughout the school year. After several sessions of working on their expressive dances in small groups, each group then presents its final product to the rest of the class. The rest of the class, as "audience," then shares its feelings as to how the structure, mood, and symbols have been captured through the body movements. Video-taping may add another dimension of observation and reflection, as children enjoy seeing their creations "immortalized" on film and can respond to their own growth in expression while reliving a piece of fondly-recalled literature.

Summary
The diverse learners in today's classrooms need equally diverse ways to express what they know and many other channels by which children can learn. A marriage of literacy and the arts provides those channels, offering activities that highlight the multiple abilities that children may possess.

Music, dance, art, and photography can all be brought into the regular classroom by affective teachers who may have little background in the arts, but who are open to allowing children to explore knowledge and respond to ideas in nontraditional ways. The arts integrated with an affective language arts program can lend joy, spontaneity, and a high degree of satisfaction to learning. Rather than merely "frills" as they were once considered, the arts are the universal language that provide a voice for EVERY child.

References

Cecil, N.L., and P. Lauritzen. *Literacy and the Arts in the Integrated Classroom: Alternative Ways of Knowing.* White Plains, NY: Longman, Inc., 1994.

Chenfield, M.B. *Teaching Language Arts Creatively.* 2nd ed. San Diego: Harcourt Brace Jovanovich, 1987.

Eeds, M., and R. Peterson. *Grand Conversations: Literature Groups in Action.* NY: Scholastic, 1990.

Faltis, C.J. *Joinfostering: Adapting Teaching Strategies for the Multilingual Classroom.* NY: Macmillan, 1993.

Gardner, H. *Frames of Mind.* NY: Basic Books, 1990.

Livo, N., and D. Cha. *Folk Stories of the Hmong.* Englewood, CO: Libraries Unlimited, 1991.

Sendak, M. *Where the Wild Things Are.* NY: Harper Junior Books, 1963.

Appendix One
Predictable Books

Predictable books: language patterns, repetitive words, phrases, questions, story patterns, cumulative tales, numerical sequences, days of week, months, hierarchies, songs, and rhymes.

Aardema, Verna, reteller. *Why Mosquitoes Buzz in People's Ears*. Illustrated by Leo and Diane Dillon. Dial, 1975.
____. *Bringing the Rain to Kapiti Plain: A Nandi Tale*. Illustrated by Beatriz Vidal. Dial, 1981.
Adams, Pam. *This Old Man*. Grossett, 1974.
Alain. *One, Two, Three, Going to the Sea*. Scholastic, 1964.
Aliki. *Go Tell Aunt Rhody*. Macmillan, 1974.
____. *Hush Little Baby*. Prentice-Hall, 1968.
____. *My Five Senses*. Crowell, 1962.
Allen, Pamela. *Bertie and the Bear*. Coward, 1984.
Asch, Frank. *Monkey Face*. Parents, 1977.
Balian, Lorna. *The Animal*. Abingdon, 1972.
____. *Where in the World is Henry?* Bradbury, 1972.
Bang, Molly. *Ten, Nine, Eight*. Greenwillow, 1983.
Barchas, Sarah E. *I Was Walking Down the Road*. Scholastic, 1975.
Barrett, Judi. *Animals Should Definitely NOT Wear Clothing*. Atheneum, 1970.
Barton, Byron. *Buzz, Buzz, Buzz*. Macmillan, 1973.
Baten, Helen, and Barbara Von Malnar. *I'm Going to Build a Supermarket One of These Days*. Holt, 1970.
Battaglia, Aurelius. *Old Mother Hubbard*. Golden, 1972.
Baum, Arline, and Joseph Baum. *One Bright Monday Morning*. Random House, 1962.
Becker, John. *Seven Little Rabbits*. Illustrated by Barbara Cooney. Walker, 1973.
Beckman, Kaj. *Lisa Cannot Sleep*. Watts, 1969.

Bellah, Melanie. *A First Book of Sounds*. Golden, 1963.

Berenstain, Stanley, and Janice Berenstain. *The B Book*. Random House, 1971.

Bishop, Gavin. *Chicken Licken*. Oxford University Press, 1985.

Bonne, Rose, and Alan Mills. *I Know an Old Lady*. Rand McNally, 1961.

Brand, Oscar. *When I First Came to this Land*. Putnam, 1974.

Brandenberg, Franz. *I Once Knew a Man*. Macmillan, 1970.

Brennan, Patricia D. *Hitchety Hatchety Up I Go!* Illustrated by Richard Royevsky. Macmillan, 1985.

Brooke, Leslie. *Johnny Crow's Garden*. Warne, 1968.

Brown, Marc. *Witches Four*. Parents, 1980.

Brown, Marcia. *The Three Billy Goats Gruff*. Harcourt, 1957.

Brown, Margaret Wise. *Four Fur Feet*. William R. Scott, 1961.

____. *The Friendly Book*. Golden, 1954.

____. *Goodnight Moon*. Harper, 1947.

____. *Home for a Bunny*. Golden, 1956.

____. *The Important Book*. Harper, 1949.

____. *Where Have You Been?* Scholastic, 1952.

Brown, Ruth. *A Dark, Dark Tale*. Dial, 1981.

Burningham, John. *Mr. Grumpy's Outing*. Holt, 1971.

____. *The Shopping Basket*. Crowell, 1980.

Cameron, Polly. *I Can't Said the Ant*. Coward, 1961.

Carle, Eric. *Do You Want to Be My Friend?* Harper, 1971.

____. *The Grouchy Ladybug*. Crowell, 1977.

____. *The Mixed-Up Chameleon*. Crowell, 1975.

____. *The Very Busy Spider*. Philomel, 1984.

____. *The Very Hungry Caterpillar*. Collins World, 1969.

Carlstrom, Nancy White. *Jesse Bear, What Will You Wear?* Illustrated by Bruce Degen. Macmillan, 1986.

Charlip, Remy. *Fortunately*. Parents, 1964.

____. *What Good Luck! What Bad Luck!* Scholastic, 1969.

Considine, Kate, and Ruby Schuler. *One, Two, Three, Four*. Holt, 1965.

Cook, Bernadine. *The Little Fish That Got Away*. Addison-Wesley, 1976.

Cummings, Pat. *Jimmy Lee Did It*. Lothrop, 1985.

de Paola, Tomie. *Tomie de Paola's Mother Goose*. Putnam, 1985.

_____. *When Everyone Was Fast Asleep*. Holiday House, 1976.

de Regniers, Beatrice Schenk. *Catch a Little Fox*. Seabury, 1970.

_____. *The Day Everybody Cried*. Viking, 1967.

_____. *How Joe Bear and Sam the Moose Got Together*. Parents, 1965.

_____. *The Little Book*. Walck, 1961.

_____. *May I Bring a Friend?* Atheneum, 1972.

_____. *Willy O'Dwyer Jumped in the Fire*. Atheneum, 1968.

Domanska, Janina. *If All the Seas Were One Sea*. Macmillan, 1971.

_____. *The Turnip*. Macmillan, 1969.

Duff, Maggie. *Johnny and His Drum*. Walck, 1972.

_____. *Rump, Pum, Pum*. Macmillan, 1978.

Eastman, P.D. *Are You My Mother?* Random House, 1960.

Einsel, Walter. *Did You Ever See?* Scholastic, 1962.

Emberley, Barbara. *Drummer Hoff*. Illustrated by Ed Emberley. Prentice-Hall, 1967.

Emberley, Barbara, and Ed Emberley. *One Wide River to Cross*. Illustrated by Ed Emberley. Scholastic, 1966.

Emberley, Ed. *Klippity Klop*. Little, Brown, 1974.

Ets, Marie Hall. *Elephant in a Well*. Viking, 1972.

_____. *Play With Me*. Viking, 1955.

Farber, Norma. *As I Was Crossing Boston Common*. Illustrated by Arnold Lobel. Dutton, 1975.

Flack, Marjorie. *Ask Mr. Bear*. Macmillan, 1932.

Flora, James. *Sherwood Walks Home*. Harcourt, 1966.

Fyleman, Rose. "The Goblin." *Picture Rhymes from Foreign Lands*. Lippincott, 1935.

Gag, Wanda. *Millions of Cats*. Faber and Faber, 1929.

Galdone, Paul. *The Gingerbread Boy*. Seabury, 1975.

_____. *Henny Penny*. Scholastic, 1968.

_____. *The Three Bears*. Scholastic, 1973.

Galdone, Paul. *The Three Billy Goats Gruff*. Seabury, 1973.

___. *The Little Red Hen*. Scholastic, 1973.

___. *The Three Little Pigs*. Clarion, 1970.

Gerstein, Mordicai. *Roll Over!* Crown, 1984.

Ginsburg, Mirra. *The Chick and the Duckling*. Macmillan, 1972.

___. *Good Morning, Chick*. Illustrated by Byron Barton. Greenwillow, 1980.

Greenberg, Polly. *Oh Lord, I Wish I Was a Buzzard*. Macmillan, 1968.

Greene, Carol. *The World's Biggest Birthday Cake*. Illustrated by Tom Dunnington. Childrens Press, 1985.

Guilfoile, Elizabeth. *Nobody Listens to Andrew*. Scholastic, 1957.

Guthrie, Donna. *The Witch Who Lived Down the Hall*. Illustrated by Amy Schwartz. Harcourt Brace Jovanovich, 1985.

Hale, Irina. *Brown Bear in a Brown Chair*. Atheneum, 1983.

Hawkins, Colin, and Jacqui Hawkins. *Old Mother Hubbard*. Putnam, 1985.

Hayes, Sara. *This Is the Bear*. Illustrated by Helen Craig. Lippincott, 1986.

Hill, Eric. *Nursery Rhyme Peek-a-Boo*. Price/Stern/Sloan, 1982.

Hoffman, Hilde. *The Green Grass Grows All Around*. Macmillan, 1968.

Howell, Lynn, and Richard Howell. *Winifred's New Bed*. Knopf, 1985.

Hutchins, Pat. *Don't Forget the Bacon*. Puffin, 1985.

___. *Good-Night, Owl!* Macmillan/Penguin, 1982.

___. *Happy Birthday, Sam*. Puffin/Penguin, 1981.

___. *Rosie's Walk*. Collier, 1968.

___. *Titch*. Collier, 1971.

___. *You'll Soon Grow into Them, Titch*. Greenwillow, 1983.

___. *1 Hunter*. Greenwillow, 1982.

Isadora, Rachel. *I Touch*. Greenwillow, 1985.

___. *I See*. Greenwillow, 1985.

___. *I Hear*. Greenwillow, 1985.

Joslin, Sesyle. *What Do You Say, Dear?* Scholastic Press, 1958.

Joyce, Irma. *Never Talk to Strangers*. Golden, 1967.

Keats, Ezra Jack. *Over in the Meadow*. Scholastic, 1971.

Kellogg, Steven. *Much Bigger than Martin*. Dial, 1976.

Kent, Jack. *The Fat Cat*. Parents, 1971.

Klein, Lenore. *Brave Daniel*. Scholastic, 1958.

Kraus, Robert. *Whose Mouse Are You?* Illustrated by Jose Aruego and Ariane Dewey. Greenwillow, 1986.

Kraus, Ruth. *Bears*. Scholastic, 1948.

_____. *The Carrot Seed*. Illustrated by Crockett Johnson. Harper, 1945.

_____. *A Hole Is to Dig*. Harper, 1952.

Kroll, Steven. *That Makes Me Mad*. Starstream, 1980.

Langstaff, John. *Frog Went A-Courtin'*. Harcourt, 1955.

_____. *Oh, A-Hunting We Will Go*. Illustrated by Nancy Winslow Parker. Atheneum, 1970.

Laurence, Ester. *We're Off to Catch a Dragon*. Abingdon, 1969.

Lexau, Joan. *Crocodile and Hen*. Harper, 1969.

Lloyd, David. *Bread and Cheese*. Illustrated by Deborah Ward. Random House, 1984.

_____. *Jack and Nelly*. Illustrated by Clive Scruton. Random House, 1984.

Lobel, Anita. *King Rooster, Queen Hen*. Greenwillow, 1975.

Lobel, Arnold. *The Rose in My Garden*. Illustrated by Anita Lobel. Greenwillow, 1984.

McGovern, Ann. *Too Much Noise*. Scholastic, 1967.

Mack, Stan. *10 Bears in My Bed*. Pantheon, 1974.

McMillan, Bruce. *Kitten Can...* Lothrop, 1984.

Mars, W.T. *The Old Woman and Her Pig*. Western, 1964.

Martin, Bill, Jr. *Brown Bear, Brown Bear, What Do You See?* Illustrated by Eric Carle. Holt, 1983.

_____. *Fire! Fire! Said Mrs. McGuire*. Holt, 1970.

_____. *A Ghost Story*. Holt, 1970.

_____. *The Haunted House*. Holt, 1970.

_____. *Old Mother Middle Muddle*. Holt, 1970.

_____. *Up and Down the Escalator*. Holt, 1970.

Marzollo, Jean. *Uproar on Hollercat Hill*. Illustrated by Steven Kellogg. Dial, 1981.

Mayer, Mercer. *If I Had...* Dial, 1968.

____. *Just For You*. Golden, 1975.

Memling, Carl. *Ten Little Animals*. Golden, 1961.

Mendoza, George. *A Wart Snake in a Fig Tree*. Dial, 1968.

Miller, Edna. *Mousekin Takes a Trip*. Prentice-Hall, 1976.

Milne, A.A. "Puppy and I," *When We Were Very Young*. Dutton, 1924.

Moffett, Martha. *A Flower Pot Is Not a Hat*. Dutton, 1972.

Most, Bernard. *If The Dinosaurs Come Back*. Harcourt, 1978.

Munari, Bruno. *The Elephant's Wish*. Philomel, 1980.

____. *Jimmy Lost His Cap, Where Can It Be?* Philomel, 1980.

Muntean, Michaela. *Bicycle Bear*. Illustrated by Doug Cushman. Parents, 1983.

Palmer, Janet. *Ten Days of School*. Bank Street College of Education, Macmillan, 1969.

Parkinson, Kathy, reteller. *The Enormous Turnip*. Whitman, 1985.

Patrick, Gloria. *A Bug in a Jug*. Scholastic, 1970.

Pearson, Tracey Campbell. *Old MacDonald Had a Farm*. Dial, 1984.

Peek, Merle, adapter. *Mary Wore Her Red Dress and Henry Wore His Green Sneakers*. Clarion, 1985.

Peppe, Rodney. *The House that Jack Built*. Delacorte, 1970.

Peterson, Jeanne Whitehouse. *While the Moon Shines Bright: A Bedtime Chant*. Illustrated by Margot Apple. Harper, 1981.

Piper, Walter. *The Little Engine That Could*. 1976.

Polushkin, Maria. *Mother, Mother, I Want Another*. Crown, 1978.

Pomerantz, Charlotte. *The Piggy in the Puddle*. Illustrated by James Marshall. Macmillan, 1974.

Preston, Edna Mitchell. *The Sad Story of the Little Bluebird and the Hungry Cat*. Illustrated by Barbara Cooney. Four Winds, 1975.

____. *Where Did My Mother Go?* Four Winds, 1978.

Quackenbush, Robert. *No Mouse for Me!* Watts, 1981.

_____. *She'll Be Comin' Round the Mountain.* Lippincott, 1973.

_____. *Skip to My Lou.* Lippincott, 1975.

Rice, Eve. *Benny Bakes a Cake.* Greenwillow, 1981.

_____. *Sam Who Never Forgets.* Greenwillow, 1977.

Rockwell, Anne. *Honk, Honk!* Dutton, 1980.

Rokoff, Sandra. *Here Is a Cat.* Singapore: Hallmark Children's Editions, n.d.

Scheer, Julian, and Marvin Bileck. *Rain Makes Applesauce.* Holiday House, 1964.

_____. *Upside Down Day.* Holiday House, 1968.

Shulevitz, Uri. *One Monday Morning.* Scribner's, 1967.

Skaar, Grace. *What Do the Animals Say?* Scholastic, 1972.

Slobodkin, Esphyr. *Caps for Sale.* Addison-Wesley, 1947.

Sonneborn, Ruth A. *Someone Is Eating the Sun.* Random House, 1974.

Spier, Peter. *The Fox Went Out on a Chilly Night: An Old Song.* Puffin, 1984.

Stanley, Diane Zuromskis. *Fiddle-I-Fee.* Little, Brown, 1979.

Stover, JoAnn. *If Everybody Did.* David McKay, 1960.

Sutton, Eve. *My Cat Likes to Hide in Boxes.* Scholastic, 1973.

Tafuri, Nancy. *Have You Seen My Duckling?* Greenwillow, 1984.

Tolstoy, Alexei. *The Great Big Enormous Turnip.* Watts, 1968.

Watanabe, Shigeo. *What a Good Lunch!* Illustrated by Yasuo Ohtomo. Philomel, 1980.

_____. *Where's My Daddy.* Philomel, 1982.

Welber, Robert. *Goodbye, Hello.* Pantheon, 1974.

Wells, Rosemary. *Noisy Nora.* Dial, 1973.

Westcott, Nadine. *I Know an Old Lady Who Swallowed a Fly.* 1980.

Wildsmith, Brian. *The Twelve Days of Christmas.* Watts, 1972.

Wolcott, Patty. *Double-Decker, Double-Decker, Double-Decker Bus.* Illustrated by Bob Barner. Addison-Wesley, 1980.

Wolkstein, Diane. *The Visit.* Knopf, 1977.

Wondriska, William. *All the Animals Were Angry.* Holt, 1970.

Wood, Audrey. *King Bidgood's in the Bathtub*. Illustrated by Don Wood. Harcourt, 1985.

____. *The Napping House*. Illustrated by Don Wood. Harcourt, 1984.

Zemach, Harve. *The Judge: An Untrue Tale*. Illustrated by Margot Zemach. Farrar, Straus, 1969.

Zemach, Margot. *The Teeny Tiny Woman*. Scholastic, 1965.

Zolotow, Charlotte. *Do You Know What I'll Do?* Harper, 1958.

Appendix Two
Two Field-Tested Units

UNIT I

Title: How Do Pioneers of Today Compare with Those of the Past?

Brief Description: A three-week unit of study geared for a third-grade class comparing pioneers of the 1800s with pioneers of today.

I.   **Major Concept:** There are many similarities between pioneers of the past and pioneers of today.

II. **Learning Goals:**
   A.   To compare and contrast the pioneers of the 1800s with those of today.
   B.   To help students evaluate the pioneers' use of resources and analyze what solutions to problems may have been possible.
   C.   To allow students to identify with several famous pioneers and explore the characteristics that made them famous.

III. **Teaching Objectives:**
   A.   To impart some factual information about these areas of pioneer life:
      1. Travel
      2. Homes
      3. Food
      4. Clothing
      5. Education
      6. Religion
      7. Social Activities

B.   To study several famous pioneers to gain perspective on what might have made them famous.

IV. List of Materials
A.   Pictures depicting frontier life
B.   Construction paper, glue, scissors, etc.
C.   Computers and software
D.   Typical pioneer clothes
E.   Small jars with lids, whipping cream, crackers, knives
F.   Records of pioneer songs

V. List of References
A.   Books
1. *American Folk Poetry* (Emrich)
2. *Pioneer Tenderfoot* (Estep)
3. *Never Miss a Sunset* (Gilge)
4. *Cowboys and Cattle Company* (American Heritage Publ.)
5. *The California Gold Rush* (American Heritage Publ.)
6. *The Pioneer Twins* (Perkins)
7. *Little House on the Prairie Series* (Wilder)
8. *Dan Frontier Series* (Hurley)
B.   Media
1. Songs of the Trail (RCA Victor)
2. 45 Songs Children Love to Sing (RCA Camden)
3. Oregon Trail (MECC)
4. The Opening of the West (filmstrip)
5. Americans Move West (picture cards)

VI. Enabling Activities
A.   Use math skills of addition and subtraction to compute distances between cities on the Oregon Trail.
B.   Hypothesize about supplies needed for a trip West.
C.   Analyze effects of natural events on the move West.

D. Learn several songs depicting pioneer life.

E. Participate in several folk dances.

F. Compare modern clothing with pioneer clothes.

G. Write a story in the person of a modern pioneer or one living in the 1800s.

H. Make butter and discuss the time and effort involved in making food this way.

I. Listen to stories about early and modern pioneers.

J. Simulate the journey West via the Oregon Trail.

K. Construct a scale model of a pioneer cabin.

L. Help to paint a mural of The Westward Journey or America's exploration of outer space.

M. Participate in a skit of either early or modern pioneer life.

N. Compose a ballad for modern pioneers.

VII. Culminating Activities

A. Hold a parent's night, featuring folk dances of the pioneers of the 1800s and the skits of early and modern pioneers.

B. Make a class book of early and modern pioneers.

C. Hold an "open house" of completed projects for other classes.

VIII. Evaluation Procedures

A. Pre- and post-test on factual information of the pioneers of the 1800s.

B. Essay discussing how early and modern pioneers are the same and different.

C. Observation of student behavior, attitude, and understandings while doing projects.

D. Student-teacher conferences on projects.

E. Creativity expressed in projects.

UNIT II

Title: What Have We Learned About Outer Space?

Brief Description: A three-week unit of study for fourth-graders concerning past and current work done in space exploration; what an astronaut does; and how rockets are designed.

I.   **Major Concept:** Valuable work has already been done in space exploration, but there are still new areas to be explored.

II. **Learning Goals:**
   A.   To compare and contrast views of outer space before and after man landed on the moon.
   B.   To value the work already done in space, and hypothesize about what the future holds for space exploration.
   C.   To identify with the feelings of astronauts as they explored outer space.

III. **Teaching Goals:**
   A.   To impart some factual information about the following areas:
      1. The earth and the planets
      2. Early space exploration
      3. The Apollo program
      4. Firing a rocket
      5. Skylab
      6. The space shuttle
   B.   To help children understand what the job of an astronaut entails and have them become familiar with several astronauts' lives.

IV. **List of Materials**
   A.   Computer and software

    B.   Rocket display
    C.   NASA patches
    D.   Paper plates
    E.   "Star Wars" music; tape recorder
    F.   Moon myths
    G.   "Mission to Mars" game
    H.   Apollo diagram
    I.   Tape of dialogue between NASA and Skylab

V. List of References
    A.   Books
        1. *Space and Beyond* (Montgomery)
        2. *Space Cat* (Marshal and Ruthven)
        3. *Barney in Space* (Goff)
        4. *First Men in Space* (Clark)
        5. *A Space Age Cookbook for Kids* (Porentea)
        6. *If You Were an Astronaut* (Moore)
        7. *SPACE: An Easy-to-Read Fact Book* (Crowley)
        8. *Space Shuttle* (Jay)
        9. *Easy to Make Spaceships that Really Fly* (Blockma)
      10. *Astronomy for Everybody* (Newcomb)
    B.   Media
       Filmstrips
       1. Moon, Sun, Stars
       2. Beyond the Solar System
       3. The Solar System
       Movies
       1. A Trip to the Moon
       2. Flash Gordon's Old Movies

VI. Enabling Activities
    A.   Complete a cumulative notebook (space log).
    B.   Build and decorate a spacecraft for a "Great Space Race."

C. Collect data at the Great Space Race and make hypotheses.
D. Label diagrams of spacecrafts.
E. Complete math warp project.
F. Play "Mission to Mars."
G. Simulate space voyage on computer.
H. Participate in gravity experiment.
I. Graph the planets.
J. Listen to tape of dialogue between NASA and Skylab.
K. Do research on astronaut of choice.
L. Complete time line of space history.

VII. **Culminating Activities**
A. Present space logs at open house.
B. Compile a classbook of astronauts researched.
C. Set off rocket in field for other classes.
D. Space Age luncheon with food eaten by astronauts.

VIII. **Evaluation Procedures**
A. Pre- and post-tests on factual information about our solar system and the space program.
B. Essay synthesizing understandings about what we have learned through space exploration.
C. Observation of student behavior, attitudes.
D. Student-teacher conferences about projects.
E. Creativity expressed in projects.

Appendix Three
Sample Learning Stations

COMPREHENSION SKILLS CENTER

Purpose of Center: To provide reinforcement experiences with comprehension skills.

RIDDLE MATCH

TASK CARD

1. READ THE RIDDLES ON THE POCKETS.

2. FIND THE ANSWERS IN THE ANSWER CARD POCKET.

3. PUT THE ANSWER CARDS IN THE RIGHT POCKETS.

4. CHECK YOUR WORK BY SEEING THAT THE NUMBER ON THE POCKET, AND THE NUMBER ON THE ANSWER CARD MATCH.

205

Materials:
>Two 14" x 20" pieces of cardboard
>Two 14" x 20" pieces of colored tagboard to cover cardboard
>One roll of masking tape to make hinges for the cardboard and to bind the edges
>Eighteen library book pockets
>Adhesive dots
>Eighteen 3" x 5" index cards

Procedure: One student reads the riddles on the library book pockets. Another student finds the answer to the riddle on one of the cards in the "Answer Pocket." The card is placed in the correct pocket.

Evaluation: Adhesive dots with numbers corresponding to the numbered dots on the library book pockets are placed on the backs of the answer cards, so the student is able to evaluate the activity.

COMICS SEQUENCE

Materials:
> Cartoon pictures which have been cut apart. These may be obtained from newspapers or comic books.
> Twenty-four 5" x 7½" envelopes
> 3" x 5" index cards for mounting comics

Procedure: The student arranges the cartoon frames in their correct sequence.

Evaluation: An answer key should be provided so that the activity is self-correcting. Symbols work well as a coding system (see illustration).

PARAGRAPH SEQUENCE

Materials:

Twenty-four 9" x 12" pieces of tagboard or cardboard

Twenty-four stories, cut into paragraphs. These may be obtained from discarded texts, children's magazines or written by the teacher and students.

Twenty-four plastic sleeves or clear contact paper to protect the materials.

Wax marking pencils

Carpet squares for erasing

Procedure: The child reads the paragraphs and numbers them in correct sequence.

Evaluation: A correcting key may be provided or a key placed on the back of each card in order to make the activity self-correcting.

MAKE THE HEADLINES

Materials:
Twenty-four 6" x 8" cards
Newspaper articles
Wax marking pencils
Carpet squares for erasing

Procedure: The student reads the article on the card and then writes a headline for the article. The actual headline is attached to the reverse side of the card.

Evaluation: Student evaluated.

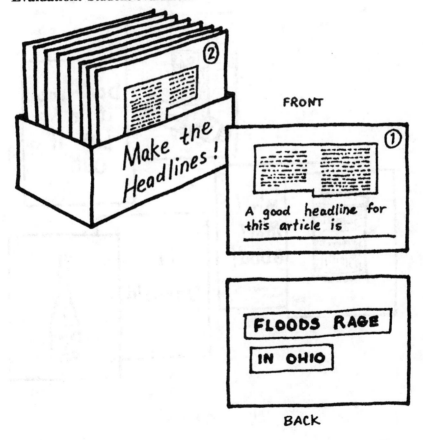

"AD CONCENTRATION"

Materials:
    Thirty or forty 3" x 5" cards
    Labels from products, magazine advertisements, etc.
    Glue

Procedure: The cards are placed face down on a table or the floor. The first player turns over any two cards; if they are a match he keeps them and continues to play until he misses. The player with the most cards at the end of the game is the winner.

Evaluation: Student evaluation or teacher observation.

PLAYER CONTRAST

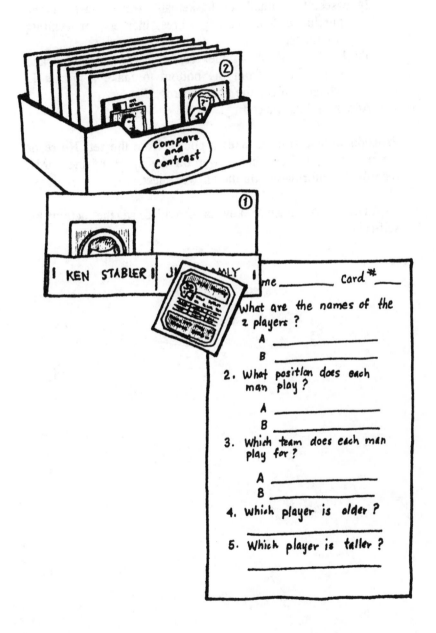

Materials:

24 baseball, football, or basketball cards. These can be purchased from variety stores, markets, or vending machines.

Twelve 5" x 8" plain index cards. These are folded and stapled 1½" from the bottom to make a pocket in which to place the player cards.

Adhesive dots for coding.

Procedure: The student takes a pocket from the set. He reads the questions, locates the answer on the backs of the cards, records the information on the answer sheet.

Evaluation: An answer key is provided so the activity is self-correcting.

WHAT'S THE STORY

Materials:
 Four ring binders or manila folders
 Pictures from magazines and newspapers
 Tagboard or construction paper for mounting pictures
 3" x 5" index cards
 Corner mounts
 Four 5" x 8" envelopes for holding story cards

Procedure: The student reads the paragraph on the index card, finds the picture that the paragraph tells about, and fits the card in the corner mounts under the picture.

Evaluation: The pictures and cards may be coded so that the activity is self-correcting.

QUESTION MATCH

Materials:
>   Five phrase cards telling WHO
>   Five phrase cards telling WHAT
>   Five phrase cards telling WHERE
>   Five phrase cards telling WHEN
>   Five phrase cards telling WHY
>   Five phrase cards telling HOW

Sixty 2¼" x 3½" cards, distribution as follows:
>   Five question cards asking WHO
>   Five question cards asking WHAT
>   Five question cards asking WHERE
>   Five question cards asking WHEN
>   Five question cards asking WHY
>   Five question cards asking HOW

Procedure: Two to four children may participate in the game. The cards are shuffled and five are placed face up in the center of the table. The first player examines the five cards to determine whether or not there is a match—a match being a phrase card that answers a question card. If there are matches, the child identifies them and picks them up, laying down other cards to fill their places. He then turns up a card from the top of the deck and determines if he can make a match. He may continue to turn up cards until he cannot make a match, in which case he places the card face up with the others. There must be five cards turned up as each player begins his turn. The player having the most cards at the end of the game is the winner.

Evaluation: Teacher observation or participation.

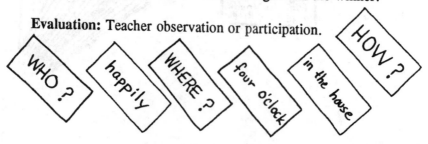

TALL TALE CENTER

Purpose of Center: To provide children with the opportunity to read and enjoy tall tale stories.

VIEWING STATION

Materials:
- One piece of cardboard, 18" x 22"
- Two pieces of cardboard, 11" x 22"
- One piece of tagboard for back cover, 18" x 22"
- Four pieces of tagboard, 11" x 18" for sides
- One piece of white tagboard, 18" x 22" for viewing screen
- Masking tape 1½" wide for hinges
- Contact paper (do not put on screen)
- Filmstrip projector
- Filmstrip
- Pencils
- Paper
- Task Cards (optional)

Procedure: Children will view filmstrip. Questions may be written on task cards or they may be asked orally.

Evaluation: Answer sheet or teacher observation.

TASK CARD

1. What does exaggeration mean?

2. Who was Paul Bunyan?

3. Write three examples of exaggeration in this story.

CREATIVE WRITING STATION

Materials:
   Three manila folders for story wheels
   Three shape books
   Pencils
   Writing paper
   Construction paper
   Scissors
   (See Fairy Tale Center)

Procedure: Child will choose one creative writing activity. If the child chooses to do a shape book, he must trace the pattern on his writing paper. After the story has been completed the child can make a shape folder for his story.

Evaluation: Teacher corrected.

STORY STARTER WHEELS

Make three 5" circles. Make three windows 2" by ¾" (see drawing for placement of windows).

Use one-inch brads to mount circles to manila folder.

On top wheel put nouns or noun phrases. On middle wheel put verb phrases and on last wheel put prepositional phrases and/or objects.

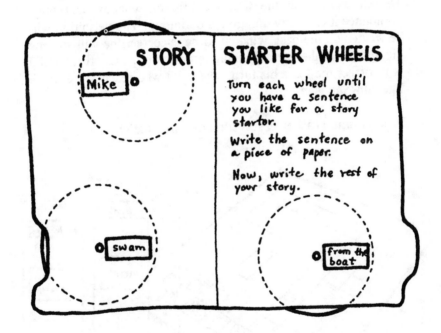

GAME STATION

Materials:
  One game board
  Vocabulary cards
  Markers
  Dice
  Three pocket windows
  Word strips

Procedure: Children will roll the die to see who starts the game. The child looks at the first word in his window and must pronounce it correctly and give a definition. The definition will be written on the back window. If he is correct, he will roll the die and move the corresponding number of spaces. If the child is incorrect, he loses his turn. The child who reaches the finish line wins the game.

Evaluation: Teacher observation or participation.

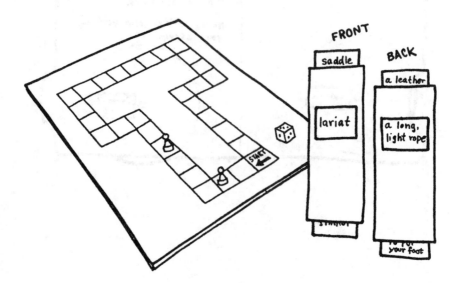

ART STATION

Materials:
   Pencils
   Crayons
   Construction paper 12" x 18"
   Task Cards

Procedure: Child will take one art task card from the box. On the task card will be written a descriptive scene from one of the tall tale stories. The child will illustrate the scene he has chosen.

Evaluation: Teacher observation.

READING CENTER

FREE READING STATION

Materials:
    Books
    Table
    Rug (if possible)
    Couch or chair (if possible)
    Pillows (if possible)

Procedure: Child will pick a book from the shelf to read.

Evaluation: Need not be evaluated.

FAIRY TALE CENTER

Purpose of Center: To provide children with the opportunity to read, listen, and dramatize the literary form of fairy tales in conjunction with English skills.

LISTENING STATION

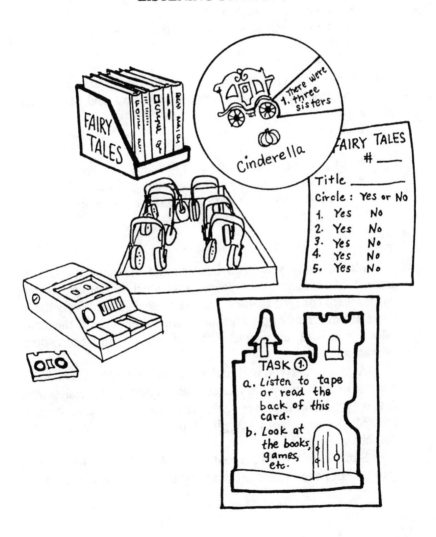

Materials:
    30 minute tape
    Tape recorder
    Books with tape
    Set of earphones
    Double 12" circles—one for each story
    Brass paper fasteners
    4¼" x 5½" ditto answer sheets
    8½" x 11" castle-shaped task card
    Pencils

Procedure: The children read the task card and follow the directions step-by-step. (See sample task card and script that follow.)

    Task Card

- Listen to tape.
- Choose a wheel about a fairy tale.
- Answer the questions on an answer sheet.
- Now, choose a story to read or listen to the tape of a story.

Tape Script

Many, many years ago most people did not have books. Instead of reading books people told stories. Sometimes the stories were changed as one man told another. That is why today there are different beginnings and different endings to the same tales. You will even find different names for the various characters.

At this center you will find some library books and some of my books with many fairy tales. Fairy tales are special stories that we read over and over again. They are fun to tell each other too. Maybe some boys and girls will write new fairy tales for our class.

Since fairy tales were told to people before we had books, you do not have to read all the fairy tales. We have some fairy tales on tape for the tape recorder. A friend may read a story to you, or you may read a story to yourself.

To help you decide what story you would like to read there are wheels of questions. Try to answer the questions on a wheel. If you cannot answer two questions correctly, then read the story.

Fairy tales are fun, so have a good time!

Evaluation: Fairy tale answer sheets.

VOCABULARY STATION

Materials:
    Carrell:
        One piece of cardboard 19" x 26"
        Two pieces of cardboard 13" x 19"
        Two pieces of colored tag 19" x 26"
        Four pieces of colored tag 13" x 19"
        One folded piece of tag 12" x 12" for pocket
        One roll 1½" masking tape
        Clear contact paper.
    Task Cards:
        5" x 8" cards
        Pencils
        Writing paper

Procedure: The child will select a task card and follow the directions. (See sample of task cards which follow.)

TASK CARD #1   Don't forget your NAME!!
You will need: Paper and pencil
Put the vocabulary words in alphabetical order. Pick 6 words. Write each word in a sentence. Put paper in folder.

TASK CARD #2   Don't forget your NAME!!
An antonym is a word having the opposite meaning of another word.
Example: hot/cold
You will need: Paper and pencil
Pick 6 vocabulary words. Write an antonym for the words you choose. Put paper in folder.

TASK CARD #3   Don't forget your NAME!!
You will need: Paper and pencil
Use the vocabulary words. A noun is a person, place, or thing. List all the nouns from the "fairy tale" vocabulary list. Draw a picture of 3 of the words you listed. Have a friend check your work. Then put in folder.

Evaluation: Teacher corrected.

SYLLABLE CHIP ACTIVITY

Materials:
   Five 10" x 10" cards, divided into 2" squares
   One box
   100 poker chips
   100 adhesive dots to label poker chips

Procedure: Child takes a word card. He says each word quietly. He counts the number of syllables he hears. He places a numbered poker chip on the word to show how many syllables it has.

Evaluation: Answer key is provided for self correction.

FAIRY TALES				
village	princess	throne	golden	fairy
tale	handsome	elf	castle	tower
enchant	prince	creature	king	fortune
kingdom	witch	magic	peddler	knight
beast	dragon	queen	treasure	robber

ANSWER KEY				
②	②	①	②	②
①	②	①	②	②
②	①	②	①	②
②	①	②	②	①
①	②	①	②	②

CREATIVE WRITING

Materials:
Two pieces of cardboard 13" x 19"
Four pieces of colored tag 13" x 19"
One folded piece of colored tag 8" x 12" for pocket
One folded piece of colored tag 12" x 12" for pocket
Clear contact paper
Six 5" x 8" cards
Masking tape
Writing paper

Procedure: The student will choose one of the story starters. The first paragraph of a fairy tale is on the card. The student will copy the paragraph and finish the story.

Evaluation: Teacher corrected.

SAVE THE PRINCESS

Materials:
> One piece of cardboard 13" x 19"
> One piece of colored tag 13" x 19"
> Clear contact paper
> Four markers
> One die
> Deck of vocabulary cards

Procedure: Children take turns rolling the die, reading a word and moving the number of spaces on the die. If a child is unable to read a word he loses a turn. The first child to the castle is the winner.

Evaluation: Teacher observation or participation.

RESEARCH CENTER

PROJECTS

1. Compare two fairy tales.

   List: Characters Vocabulary Events

   _____

   How are they alike?

   _____

   How are they different?

   _____

2. Make a world map of fairy tales.

Materials:
   Chart paper (18" x 22" approximately)
   Writing paper
   Pencils
   Crayons
   Colored pencils
   Printed flat world map

Procedure: Student selects a project. Research may be done both in class and at home.

Evaluation: Student presents project orally to class or to teacher.

Index